RESOLUTIONS AND STATEMENTS OF
THE UNITED NATIONS SECURITY COUNCIL (1946–2000)

NIJHOFF LAW SPECIALS

VOLUME 50

The titles published in this series are listed at the end of this volume.

Resolutions and Statements of the United Nations Security Council (1946–2000)

A Thematic Guide

Edited by

Karel Wellens

KLUWER LAW INTERNATIONAL
THE HAGUE / LONDON / NEW YORK

A C.I.P. Catalogue record for this book is available from the Library of Congress.

ISBN 90-411-1722-9

Published by Kluwer Law International,
P.O. Box 85889, 2508 CN The Hague, The Netherlands.

Sold and distributed in North, Central and South America
by Kluwer Law International,
101 Philip Drive, Norwell, MA 02061, U.S.A.

In all other countries, sold and distributed
by Kluwer Law International,
P.O. Box 85889, 2508 CN The Hague, The Netherlands.

Printed on acid-free paper

Kluwer Law International incorporates the imprint of
Martinus Nijhoff Publishers.

Printed in the Netherlands.

TABLE OF CONTENTS

LIST OF ABBREVIATIONS

AF.	Africa
AS.	Asia
C.E.E.	Central and Eastern Europe
C.L.A.C.	Central and Latin America and the Carribean
G.	General
M.E.	The Middle East
PAL.	The Palestine Question
W.E.	Western Europe

INTRODUCTION

by the editor Karel Wellens

1 THE PURPOSE

When preparing lectures, in the spring of 1988, I was struck by the fact that collecting Security Council resolutions on one particular issue, throughout UN history – in order to analyse and compare their ever changing formulation – was a rather cumbersome and time-consuming operation, even if the numbers and dates of a series of resolutions were available. Every international lawyer – whether a diplomat, practitioner, student or researcher – inevitably had to consult the annual publication "Resolutions and Decisions of the Security Council", which fortunately contains a subject matter classification and a chronological checklist as well. To my surprise, a publication containing Security Council resolutions over the years, but classified on a topic basis, was not available, at least not to my knowledge; so perhaps the time had come to make an attempt to fill this gap.

The main purpose of this publication is basically to provide international lawyers looking for the texts of resolutions and statements of the Security Council on a particular topic with a useful, thematic guide containing the essential tools, presented in a chronological order, but classified on a topic basis to help us find and compare the English and French texts electronically through the UN home page. The user of this book should then be able to immediately start on the real and important tasks ahead: to take part in negotiations, to write papers or to prepare lectures, to carry out some real, thorough legal research based upon a comparative analysis, and perhaps even to draft opinions or judgments, on both the national and international level.

In the meantime, two editions of this work appeared in bookform, and the time had come to bring out a new edition. As the ever increasing number of Security Council resolutions and statements is nowadays easily available through the UN home page (http://www.un.org/documents/), it was decided to bring out a thematic guide in this amended form without the texts of the resolutions and statements being reproduced. Although a CD-ROM could be updated regularly and could contain a much larger number of texts than a book ever could, its potential usefulness for our purposes has been overtaken by new technological developments.

The sheer expansion of Security Council activity during the last decade made it virtually impossible to include in this publication updated introductory notes introducing the topic at hand in the most neutral and objective way possible.

2 THE KIND OF MATERIAL COLLECTED

Traditionally, international lawyers wish to have before them all the necessary material before embarking upon their practical and/or academic analysis. Dealing with Security Council activities inevitably leads to the recognition that it is sometimes necessary, in order to make any valuable assessment of the Council's performance, to look at statements as well. There is an ever-increasing tendency to resort to this kind of instrument; the statements are read out by the President of the Security Council on behalf of the members of the Council[1] preceded by all kinds of formulae (expressing their views on the matter; expressing or representing the consensus of the members; which had been agreed upon or had been adopted by consensus following consultations; representing the agreement, etc.). Security Council members give preference to such statements, because of the complexity of the issue at stake, or as a preparation or a temporary substitute for the adoption of a resolution.

The role played by these "Presidential statements" in the Council's handling of a particular problem cannot be underestimated, and certainly should never be overlooked. So it would be useful to have these statements collected as well, and to have them classified in the same way as the resolutions they are coupled with. Statements of a merely procedural nature have in principle been omitted.[2]

---

1 In such cases it is abundantly clear that the President "also represents the council in its capapcity as an organ of the United Nations, although always under the authority of the Security Council (Rule 19)", S.D. Bailey, The Procedure of the UN Security council, 2nd edition, Clarendon Press, Oxford, 1988, at p. 99.

2 The same goes for the "decisions" of the Security Council listed in the aforementioned annual publications "Resolutions and Decisions fo the Security Council", because of their overwhelmingly procedural nature (e.g. a decision concerning an invitation to take part in the debate). On the term "decisions" of the Security Council, see S. Bailey, op.

Of course, the Security Council's involvement in matters of international peace and security has been far more extensive than is actually shown by the adoption of resolutions and statements. Indeed, situations, incidents, and disputes do not always have to lead to a request to the Security Council to consider the matter; in the majority of cases – depending upon a number of variable factors and surrounding circumstances – the States or parties concerned limit themselves to a request to have their letter circulated as Security Council document, certainly for the time being. These matters do not even reach the stage of debating their possible inclusion in the Council's agenda.

The very inclusion of a particular issue in the agenda could very well give rise to a real debate, dealing (partly) in fact with the heart of the matter itself. If, once the item has been put on the agenda, the ensuing discussion has not resulted in the adoption of a resolution, the topic is not retained. This is done in spite of the fact that the issues involved could very well turn out to be of great importance for peace and security and occupy a prominent place in history and in the current state of international relations. Only items the discussion of which resulted in the adoption of a resolution have been collected, in order to maintain this publication within reasonable and useful limits.

3 THE CLASSIFICATION OF THE MATERIAL

The main problem during the preparation of this work was not so much the collection of the material involved or even the drafting of the introductory notes (see paragraph 4). I was confronted with a number of semantic problems such as: what kind of useful headings should be used, given the purpose of this work? A topical classification of resolutions and statements seemed self-evident, but along which lines? And this in turn was a question closely linked and raised by the issue of the wording "items on the agenda of the Security Council".

In the early years, the description used when items were actually put on the agenda really revealed the core of the matter. Later on, a practice steadily evolved to simply refer, in a less clear way of course, to the date and origin of the letter which has led the Security Council to put the matter on its agenda. It is the general view that this method of dealing with the description of topics is not very helpful to those wanting to consult relevant resolutions and statements. As far as the titles of the topics are concerned, I have tried to use

---

cit. at pp. 236-237.

formulae which indicate, if possible, the substance of the matter which is frequently commonly referred to under that heading.

Sometimes the official description of an item has been changed over the years; this is reflected in the heading of the topic. But the Security Council has not always been very consistent in using particular descriptions or in dividing an item into several sub-items. Furthermore, the question was how to deal with large and important issues, such as South Africa or the Middle East or the Former Yugoslavia. Generally, I did follow as closely as possible the official titles of the sub-items concerned, while preferring, however, to introduce some further subdivisions if they were felt to be logical, non-controversial as such and were required for the instrumental purpose of this publication. This was obvious the case, for instance, with regard to Lebanon where a subdivision was made between the general situation in the country and the UNIFIL operations. The international lawyer's need for quick and practical access to the material had been my overriding concern in this regard.

On the other hand, there was no need to depart from the distinction used in the annual publication of Resolutions and Decisions of the Security Council between questions considered by the Security Council under its responsibility for the maintenance of international peace and security (Part I) and other matters considered by the Security Council (Part II).

There still remained the problem of the main division with regard to the topics included in part I; I had to bring some kind of order to the vast amount (107) of headings. A division along the lines of matters of substance or gravity would have been arbitrary and perhaps not very useful. So I opted for a gross geographical classification, based upon the distribution of UN members by region, adding a small number of more general issues, not directly linked to a particular region or one State.

4 How to use this Thematic Guide

As described in paragraph 3 the information is divided into two main parts: Part I, matters concerning the maintenance of international peace and security; and Part II, other matters considered by the Security Council. The next division is a geographical one, each geographical region being subdivided into numbered topics. The *corpus* of this Thematic Guide consists of an Analytical Table of Resolutions, Statements and Letters.

Each topic is built up from the same elements, in which a system of typographical indicators is applied for the sake of easy reference:

1 A thematic code, indicating the (abbreviated) geographical region and the number of the issue thereunder, e.g., AS. 08.
2 The heading.
3 A running heading, which is identical to the thematic code.
4 A list of meetings of the Security Council when the item was (placed) on the agenda or when a debate was held on its inclusion. The meetings during which a resolution has been adopted are in bold print.
5 Presidential statements if any.

In order to improve the accessibility of the resolutions the following aids are provided for the user: Annex I is a chronological list of the resolutions with their number and date and thematic code. Together, the Analytical Table of Contents and Annex I provide every possible entry. Annex II gives the composition of the Security Council (1946-2000).

5 Acknowledgments

The publication of this Thematic Guide called for assistance of several others to whom I wish to express my thanks.

The collection of resolutions, statements, meetings, results of voting would have been impossible without the help of two of my students, Ms. Marja Peters and Ms. Edith Schoots: in different stages of the preparation they undertook the necessary but monastic job of checking and double-checking the large amount of material, joined in the final stage by their colleague Ms. Monja van de Berg.

I also wish to express my most sincere thanks to Ms. Judith Smeets, who took care of the technical preparation of this publication: her assistance, provided with patience and kindness, was invaluable to me.

On numerous occasions it was comforting to be able to rely on the kind and accurate co-operation of Mr. F.A. Steenbergen, the official in charge of the International Documentation Division at the Dutch Ministry for Foreign Affairs and his successor Mrs. A.T.M. ter Horst; I wish to express my sincere thanks to both of them.

Of course only the author is responsible for every mistake in this volume. I would therefore be grateful to all those who would be so kind as to inform me of any gaps, faults, or omissions which they may notice when using this instrument in their legal profession as a diplomat, practitioner, student or researcher, in order to improve the usefulness of this Thematic Guide.

The current guide includes references to Resolutions, Statements and Letters up to 31 December 2000.

PART I

QUESTIONS CONSIDERED BY THE SECURITY COUNCIL UNDER ITS RESPONSIBILITY FOR THE MAINTENANCE OF INTERNATIONAL PEACE AND SECURITY

1

GENERAL

G. 01 Question of relations between the great powers

Meetings: **1960**: 857, 858, 859, 860, 861, 862, **863**, 880, 881, 882, 883, 893, 894, 895.

Resolution 135 (1960) of 27 May 1960

G. 02 Question relating to measures to safeguard non-nuclear-weapons states parties to the treaty on non-proliferation of nuclear weapons

Meetings: **1968**: 1430, 1431, **1433**.

Resolution 255 (1968) of 19 June 1968

G. 03 The question of hostage taking and abduction

Meetings: **1985**: **2637**
1989: **2872**

Resolution 579 (1985) of 18 December 1985
Resolution 638 (1989) of 31 July 1989

Statement, 28 January 1987
Statement, 31 July 1989

K. Wellens (ed.),
Resolutions and Statements of the United Nations Security Council (1946-2000), 3–10.

G. 04 Marking of plastic or sheet explosives for the purposes of detection

Meetings: **1989**: **2869**.

Resolution 635 (1989) of 14 June 1989

Statement, 30 December 1988

G. 05 The 40th anniversary of the first meeting of the Security Council and the inauguration on 1 January 1986 of the International Year of Peace

Statement, 17 January 1986

G. 06 United Nations Peace-keeping Operations

Statement, 30 May 1990

G. 07 The responsibility of the Security Council in the maintenance of international peace and security

Meetings: **1992**: 3046
1998: 3881, 3888, **3890**
1999: **4053**
2000: 4242, 4243

Resolution 1172 (1998) of 6 June 1998
Resolution 1269 (1999) of 19 October 1999

Statement, 6 December 1992
Statement, 31 January 1992
Statement, 14 May 1998
Statement, 29 May 1998
Statement, 6 December 2000

Letter dated 20 February 1998 from the Secretary-General addressed to the President of the Security Council

Letter dated 8 July 1998 from the Secretary-General addressed to the President of the Security Council

G. 08 An Agenda for peace: Preventive Diplomacy, Peacemaking and Peacekeeping

Meetings: **1992**: 3089, 3128, 3154
1993: 3166, 3178, 3190, 3207, 3225
1994: 3408, 3448, 3449, 3372
1995: 3492, 3492 (Resumption 1), 3492 (Resumption 2), 3503, 3609, 3611
1996: 3645

Statement, 30 June 1992
Statement, 29 October 1992
Statement, 30 November 1992
Statement, 30 December 1992
Statement, 28 January 1993
Statement, 26 February 1993
Statement, 31 March 1993
Statement, 30 April 1993
Statement, 28 May 1993
Statement, 3 May 1994
Statement, 27 July 1994
Statement, 4 November 1994
Statement, 22 February 1995
Statement, 19 December1995
Statement, 28 March 1996

Letter dated 20 January 1994 from the President of the Security Council addressed to the Secretary-General

G. 09 Security Council Action regarding acts of terrorism. Threats to peace and security by international terrorist acts

Meetings: **1998**: **3915**

Resolution 1189 (1992) of 13 August 1998

Statement, 31 January 1992
Statement, 29 July 1994
Statement, 24 January 1995
Statement, 4 March 1996

G. 10 Commemoration of the end of the Second World War in Europe
Commemoration of the end of the Second World War in the Asia-Pacific region

Meetings: **1995**: 3532, 3565

Statement, 9 May 1995
Statement, 15 August 1995

G. 11 The proposal by China, France, the Russian Federation, The United Kingdom and the United States of America on security assurances

Meetings: **1995**: **3514**

Resolution 984 (1995) of 11 April 1995

G. 12 The fiftieth anniversary of the United Nations

Meetings: **1995**: 3583

Statement, 26 September 1995

G. 13 Demining in the context of the United Nations Peacekeeping

Meetings: **1996**: 3689, 3693

Statement, 30 August 1996

G. 14 Security of United Nations Operations

Meetings: **1993**: **3283**
1997: 3750

Resolution 868 (1993) of 29 September 1993

Statement, 12 March 1997

G. 15 United Nations Peacekeeping: Dag Hammerskjöld Medal

Meetings: **1997**: **3802**

Resolution 1121 (1997) of 22 July 1997

Statement, 22 July 1997

G. 16 Protection for humanitarian assistance to refugees and others in conflict situations

Meetings: **1997**: 3778, 3778 (Resumption 1) 3790
1998: 3932, 3933, 3942

Statement, 19 June 1997
Statement, 29 September 1998

G. 17 Civilian police in peacekeeping operations

Meetings: **1997**: 3801

Statement, 14 July 1997

G. 18 Children and armed conflict
Reports of the Secretary-General on the implementation of Security Council Resolution 1261 (1999)

Meetings: **1998**: 3896, 3897
1999: 4037, **4037** (Resumption 1)
2000: 4176, **4185**

Resolution 1261 (1999) of 25 August 1999
Resolution 1314 (2000) of 11 August 2000

Statement, 29 June 1998

G. 19 Maintenance of peace and security and post-conflict peace-building. Disarmement, demobilization and reintegration of ex-combatants in a peacekeeping environment
Report of the Secretary-General on the role of the UN peacekeeping in disarmement, demobilisation and reintegration.

Meetings: **1998**: 3954, 3954 (Resumption), 3961
1999: 4020, 4020 (Resumption 1), 4021
2000: 4118, 4119

Statement, 29 December 1998
Statement, 8 July 1999
Statement, 23 March 2000

G. 20 Protection of civilians in armed conflict

Meetings: **1999**: 3977, 3978, 3980, 3980 (Resumption), 4046, 4046 (Resumption 1), **4046 (Resumption 2)**
2000: 4130, **4130 (Resumption 1)**

Resolution 1265 (1999) of 17 September 1999
Resolution 1296 (2000) of 19 April 2000

Statement, 12 February 1999

Presidential Note, 11 November 1999

Letter dated 14 February 2000 from the President of the Security Council addressed to the President of the General Assembly

G. 21 Small arms

Meetings: **1999**: 4048

Statement, 24 September 1999

G. 22 Role of the Security Council in the prevention of armed conflict

Meetings: **1999**: 4072, 4072 (Resumption), 4073
2000: 4174, 4174 (Resumption 1)

Statement, 30 November 1999
Statement, 20 July 2000

G. 23 Protection of UN personnel, associated personnel and humanitarian personnel in conflict zones.

Meetings: **2000**: 4100, 4100 (Resumption 1)

Statement, 9 February 2000

G. 24 Maintaining peace and security:humanitarian aspects of issues before the Security Council

Meetings: **2000**: 4109, 4109 (Resumption 1), 4110

Statement, 9 March 2000

G. 25 General issues relating to sanctions

Meetings: **2000**: 4128

Presidential Note, 17 April 2000

Letter dated from the Permanent Members of the Security Council dated 13 April 1995 addressed to the President of the Security-Council on the humanitarian aspects of sanctions.

G. 26 The responsibility of the Security Council in the maintenance of international peace and security. HIV/AIDS and international peacekeeping operations.

Meetings: **2000**: **4172**

Resolution 1308 (2000) of 17 July 2000

G. 27 Women and peace and Security

Meetings: **2000**: 4208, 4208 (Resumption 1), 4208 (Resumption 2), **4213**

Resolution 1325 (2000) of 31 October 2000

G. 28 Ensuring an effective role of the Security Council in the maintenance of International Peace and Security
Letter dated 10 November 2000 from the Chairman of the Security Council Working Group on the Brahmi Report addressed to the President of the Security Council

Meetings: **2000**: **4220**

Resolution 1327 (2000) of 13 November 2000

2

WESTERN EUROPE

W.E. 01 The Spanish question

Meetings: **1946**: 32, 34, 35, 36, 37, 38, **39**, 44, 45, 46, 47, 48, **49, 79**

Resolution 4 (1946) of 29 April 1946
Resolution 7 (1946) of 26 June 1946
Resolution 10 (1946) of 4 November 1946

W.E. 02 The Greek question

Meetings: **1946**: 2, 6, 7, 8, 10, 58, 59, 60, 61, 62, 64, 65, 66, 67, 68, 69, 70, **82**, 83, 84, 85, 86, **87.**
1947: 100, **101**, 123, 126, 128, 129, 130, **131**, 133, 134, 135, 136, 137, 147, 148, 150, 151, 153, 156, 158, 159, 160, 161, 162, 163, 164, 165, 166, 167, 168, 169, 170, 174, 176, **177**, 178, 180, 183, 188, **202**.

Resolution 12 (1946) of 10 December 1946
Resolution 15 (1946) of 19 December 1946
Resolution 17 (1947) of 10 February 1947
Resolution 23 (1947) of 18 April 1947
Resolution 28 (1947) of 6 August 1947
Resolution 34 (1947) of 15 September 1947

Statement, 20 September 1946

K. Wellens (ed.),
Resolutions and Statements of the United Nations Security Council (1946-2000), 11–12.

W.E. 03 The free territory of Trieste

Meetings: **1947**: 88, 89, **91**, 143, 144, 155, 203, 223.

Resolution 16 (1947) of 10 January 1947

W.E. 04 Complaint by France and the United Kingdom against Egypt
Complaint by Egypt against France and the United Kingdom

Meetings: **1956**: 734, 735, 736, 737, 738, 739, 740, 741, 742, **743**, 750, **751**.

Resolution 118 (1956) of 13 October 1956
Resolution 119 (1956) of 31 October 1956

W.E. 05 Complaint by Greece against Turkey

Meetings: **1976**: 1949, 1950, **1953**.

Resolution 395 (1976) of 25 August 1976

3

CENTRAL AND EASTERN EUROPE

C.E.E. 01 The Corfu Channel incidents

Meetings: **1947**: 95, 96, 97, 107, 109, 111, **114**, 120, 121, 122, 125, **127**.

Resolution 19 (1947) of 27 February 1947
Resolution 22 (1947) of April 1947

C.E.E. 02 The situation in Hungary

Meetings: **1956**: 746, 752, 753, **754**.

Resolution 120 (1956) of 4 November 1956

C.E.E. 03 The situation relating to Yugoslavia*
The situation in the Former Yugoslavia
The situation in Bosnia and Herzegovina
The United Nations Protection Force (UNPROFOR)

* Given the turmoil of events occuring in the region as from the summer of 1991, it was hardly suprising that the sheer peace of events and the unique complexity of the situation in the former Yugoslavia was not reflected in the description of items and sub-items discussed by the Security Council. As a result a clear-cut, useful delineation of resolutions and statements into justifiable and manageable categories has proven to be highly problematic; the Council's own inconsistency in labelling the items exacerbated the probelm. In order to keep the thematic guide as user–friendly as possible the resolutions and statements have been listed under several more general headings. A number of remaining rather smaller items which lend themselves more easily to separate listing, have been reproduced accordingly.

K. Wellens (ed.),
Resolutions and Statements of the United Nations Security Council (1946-2000), 13–30.

Reports of the Secretary-General on the United Nations Mission in Bosnia and Herzegovina (UNMIBH)
Briefing by Mr. Karl Bildt, Special Envoy of the Secretary General for the Balkans
Briefing by Mr. W. Petrisch, High Representative for the Implementation of the Peace Agreement on Bosnia and Herzegovina.

Meetings: **1991**: **3009, 3018, 3023**
1992: 3027, **3028, 3049, 3055, 3066,** 3068, 3070, **3075, 3082, 3083, 3086, 3087, 3088, 3093,** 3097, 3100, 3103, **3104, 3106,** 3111, 3113, **3114, 3118, 3119, 3122**, 3132, **3133,** 3134, 3135, 3136, **3137,** 3146, **3150**
1993: 3160, 3164, 3173, **3174,** 3176, 3177, 3180, 3184, 3186, **3189, 3191,** 3192, **3200, 3248, 3284, 3285, 3286**
1994: **3356, 3369, 3434,** 3416, **3480**
1995: **3512, 3543,** 3568, 3585, 3586, **3591, 3595**
1996: 3647, 3687, **3700,** 3701, **3723**
1997: 3740, 3749, **3760, 3776, 3787,** 3842, **3842 (Resumption)**
1998: 3862, **3883, 3892, 3909**
1999: **4014, 4030,** 4058, 4062, 4069
2000: 4105, 4117, 4136, **4162,** 4164, 4164 (Resumption 1), 4169, 4188, 4209, 4222, 4245

Resolution 713 (1991) of 25 September 1991
Resolution 721 (1991) of 27 November 1991
Resolution 724 (1991) of 15 December 1991
Resolution 727 (1992) of 8 January 1992
Resolution 740 (1992) of 7 February 1992
Resolution 743 (1992) of 21 February 1992
Resolution 749 (1992) of 7 April 1992
Resolution 752 (1992) of 15 May 1992
Resolution 757 (1992) of 30 May 1992
Resolution 758 (1992) of 8 June 1992
Resolution 760 (1992) of 18 June 1992
Resolution 761 (1992) of 29 June 1992
Resolution 762 (1992) of 30 June 1992
Resolution 764 (1992) of 13 July 1992
Resolution 769 (1992) of 7August 1992

Resolution 770 (1992) of 13 August 1992
Resolution 771 (1992) of 13 August 1992
Resolution 776 (1992) of 14 September 1992
Resolution 779 (1992) of 6 October 1992
Resolution 780 (1992) of 6 October 1992
Resolution 781 (1992) of 9 October 1992
Resolution 786 (1992) of 10 November 1992
Resolution 787 (1992) of 16 November 1992
Resolution 798 (1993) of 18 December 1992
Resolution 807 (1993) of 19 February 1993
Resolution 815 (1993) of 30 March 1993
Resolution 816 (1993) of 31 March 1993
Resolution 820 (1993) of 18 April 1993
Resolution 847 (1993) of 30 June 1993
Resolution 869 (1993) of 30 September 1993
Resolution 870 (1993) of 1 October 1993
Resolution 871 (1993) of 4 October 1993
Resolution 908 (1994) of 31 March 1994
Resolution 914 (1994) of 27 April 1994
Resolution 947 (1994) of 30 September 1994
Resolution 967 (1994) of 14 December 1994
Resolution 981 (1995) of 31 March 1995
Resolution 982 (1995) of 31 March 1995
Resolution 983 (1995) of 31 March 1995
Resolution 998 (1995) of 16 June 1995
Resolution 1019 (1995) of 9 November 1995
Resolution 1021 (1995) of 22 November 1995
Resolution 1022 (1995) of 22 November 1995
Resolution 1074 (1996) of 12 December 1996
Resolution 1088 (1997) of 31 March 1997
Resolution 1103 (1997) of 16 May 1997
Resolution 1107 (1997) of 12 June 1997
Resolution 1112 (1997) of 12 June 1997
Resolution 1144 (1997) of 19 December 1997
Resolution 1168 (1998) of 21 May 1998
Resolution 1174 (1998) of 15 June 1998
Resolution 1184 (1998) of 16 July 1998
Resolution 1247 (1999) of 18 June 1999

Resolution 1256 (1999) of 3 August 1999
Resolution 1305 (2000) of 21 June 2000

Statement, 7 January 1992
Statement, 10 April 1992
Statement, 24 April 1992
Statement, 5 May 1992
Statement, 9 July 1992
Statement, 17 July 1992
Statement, 24 july 1992
Statement, 4 August 1992
Statement, 4 August 1992
Statement, 2 September 1992
Statement, 9 September 1992
Statement, 30 October 1992
Statement, 2 December 1992
Statement, 9 December 1992
Statement, 8 January 1993
Statement, 8 January 1993
Statement, 25 January 1993
Statement, 17 February 1993
Statement, 24 February 1993
Statement, 25 February 1993
Statement, 3 March 1993
Statement, 17 March 1993
Statement, 25 March 1993
Statement, 3 April 1993
Statement, 8 April 1993
Statement, 14 September 1993
Statement, 11 August 1994
Statement, 19 August 1995
Statement, 6 October 1995
Statement, 8 August 1996
Statement, 10 October 1996
Statement, 14 February 1997
Statement, 11 March 1997
Statement, 19 March 1998
Statement, 13 July 2000

Letter dated 29 July 1993 from the Secretary-General addressed to the President of the Security Council.

Letter dated 2 August 1993 from the the President of the Security Council addressed to the Secretary-General.

Letter dated 18 August 1993 from the Secretary-General addressed to the President of the Securtiy Council.

Letter dated 20 August 1993 from the President of the Security Council addressed to the Secretary-General

Letter dated 11 Janaury 1996 from the President of the Security Council addressed to the Secretary-General

Letter dated 5 May 1997 from het Secretary addressed to the President of the Security Council.

C.E.E. 04 The Situation in the Republic of Bosnia and Herzegovina
The Situation prevailing in and around the safe area of Bihac

Meetings: **1993**: **3199**, 3201, 3202, 3203, **3208**, 3210, **3228**, **3234**, **3241**, 3247, 3257, **3269**, 3276, 3308
1994: 3327, 3333, 3336, 3336 (Resumption 1), 3336 (Resumption 2), 3336 (Resumption 3), **3344**, 3349, 3359, 3364, **3367**, 3370, 3374, 3380, 3387, 3399, 3421, **3428**, 3433, 3454, 3454 (Resumption 1), 3454 (Resumption 2), 3456, 3460, **3461**, **3462**, 3466, 3471, 3475, 3478
1995: 3486, **3487**, 3501, 3520, **3521**, **3522**, 3530, 3548, **3551**, **3553**, 3554, 3556, 3557, **3564**, 3568, 3572, 3575, 3576, **3578**, 3580, **3581**, 3587, **3601**, 3603, **3607**, **3612**, **3613**

Resolution 819 (1993) of 16 April 1993
Resolution 824 (1993) of 6 May 1993
Resolution 836 (1993) of 4 June 1993
Resolution 838 (1993) of 10 June 1993
Resolution 844 (1993) of 18 June 1993

Resolution 859 (1993) of 24 August 1993
Resolution 900 (1994) of 4 March 1994
Resolution 913 (1994) of 22 April 1994
Resolution 941 (1994) of 23 September 1994
Resolution 942 (1994) of 23 September 1994
Resolution 943 (1994) of 23 September 1994
Resolution 958 (1994) of 19 November 1994
Resolution 959 (1994) of 19 November 1994
Resolution 970 (1995) of 12 January 1995
Resolution 987 (1995) of 19 April 1995
Resolution 988 (1995) of 21 April 1995
Resolution 1003 (1995) of 5 July 1995
Resolution 1004 (1995) of 12 July 1995
Resolution 1010 (1995) of 10 August 1995
Resolution 1015 (1995) of 15 September 1995
Resolution 1016 (1995) of 21 September 1995
Resolution 1026 (1995) of 30 November 1995
Resolution 1031 (1995) of 15 December 1995
Resolution 1034 (1995) of 21 December 1995
Resolution 1035 (1995) of 21 December 1995

Statement, 21 April 1993
Statement, 21 April 1993
Statement, 10 May 1993
Statement, 22 July 1993
Statement, 14 September 1993
Statement, 28 October 1993
Statement, 9 November 1993
Statement, 9 November 1993
Statement, 7 January 1994
Statement, 3 February 1994
Statement, 14 March 1994
Statement, 6 April 1994
Statement, 14 April 1994
Statement, 4 May 1994
Statement, 25 May 1994
Statement, 1 June 1994
Statement, 30 June 1994

Statement, 2 September 1994
Statement, 30 September 1994
Statement, 13 November 1994
Statement, 18 November 1994
Statement, 26 November 1994
Statement, 29 November 1994
Statement, 13 December 1994
Statement, 6 January 1995
Statement, 17 February 1995
Statement, 14 April 1995
Statement, 3 May 1995
Statement, 3 May 1995
Statement, 14 May 1995
Statement, 23 June 1995
Statement, 14 July 1995
Statement, 20 July 1995
Statement, 25 July 1995
Statement, 19 August 1995
Statement, 7 September 1995
Statement, 8 September 1995
Statement, 18 September 1995
Statement, 12 October 1995
Statement, 7 December 1995
Statement, 4 April 1996

Letter dated 7 July 1993 from the President of the Security Council addressed to the Secretary-General

Letter dated 25 February 1994 from the President of the Security Council addressed to the Secretary-General

Letter dated 29 April 1994 from the President of the Security Council addressed to the Secretary-General

Letter dated 7 July 1994 from the President of the Security Council addressed to the Secretary-General.

C.E.E 05 The situation in Croatia
The situation prevailing in and adjacent to the United Nations Protected Areas in Croatia
Reports of the Secretary-General on the situation of Human Rights in Croatia pursuant to Resolution 1019 (1995)
Reports of the Secretary-General on the United Nations Observers Mission in Prevlaka (UNMOP)
Reports of the Secretary-General on the United Naions Transitional Administration for Eastern Slavonia, Baranja and Western Sirmium (UNTAES)
Reports of the Secretary-General on the United Nations Police Support Group

Meetings: **1993**: **3163,** 3165, 3231, 3255, 3260, 3275
1995: 3491, 3498, **3527,** 3529, 3531, **3537,** 3545, 3560, 3561, **3563,** 3573, 3584, **3596, 3600,** 3615
1996: 3617, **3619, 3626,** 3633, 3666, 3677, 3678, **3681, 3686,** 3688, 3697, **3712,** 3727, **3731**
1997: 3737, 3746, 3753, 3772, 3775, **3800,** 3818, 3824, **3843**
1998: **3847,** 3854, 3859, 3901, **3907,** 3941
1999: **3966, 4023**
2000: **4088, 4170**

Resolution 802 (1993) of 25 January 1993
Resolution 990 (1995) of 28 April 1995
Resolution 994 (1995) of 17 May 1995
Resolution 1009 (1995) of 10 August 1995
Resolution 1023 (1995) of 22 November 1995
Resolution 1025 (1995) of 30 November 1995
Resolution 1037 (1996) of 15 January 1996
Resolution 1038 (1996) of 15 January 1996
Resolution 1043 (1996) of 31 January 1996
Resolution 1066 (1996) of 15 July 1996
Resolution 1069 (1996) of 30 July 1996
Resolution 1079 (1996) of 15 November 1996
Resolution 1093 (1997) of 14 January 1997
Resolution 1119 (1997) of 14 July 1997
Resolution 1120 (1997) of 14 July 1997

Resolution 1145 (1997) of 19 November 1997
Resolution 1147 (1998) of 13 November 1998
Resolution 1183 (1998) of 15 July 1998
Resolution 1222 (1999) of 15 January 1999
Resolution 1252 (1999) of 15 July 1999
Resolution 1285 (2000) of 13 January 2000
Resolution 1307 (2000) of 13 July 2000

Statement, 27 January 1993
Statement, 8 June 1993
Statement, 15 July 1993
Statement, 30 July 1993
Statement, 14 September 1993
Statement, 17 January 1995
Statement, 7 February 1995
Statement, 1 May 1995
Statement, 4 May 1995
Statement, 16 June 1995
Statement, 3 August 1995
Statement, 4 August 1995
Statement, 7 September 1995
Statement, 3 October 1995
Statement, 22 December 1995
Statement, 8 January 1996
Statement, 23 February 1996
Statement, 22 May 1996
Statement, 3 July 1996
Statement, 3 July 1996
Statement, 15 August 1996
Statement, 20 September 1996
Statement, 20 December 1996
Statement, 31 January 1997
Statement, 7 March 1997
Statement, 19 March 1997
Statement, 25 April 1997
Statement, 8 May 1997
Statement, 18 September 1997
Statement, 20 October 1997

Statement, 13 February 1998
Statement, 6 March 1998
Statement, 2 July 1998
Statement, 6 November 1998

Letter dated 2 August 1996 from the Secretary-General addressed to the President of the Security Council

Letter dated 21 January 1997 from the Secretary-General addressed to the President of the Security Council

Letter dated 29 April 1997 from the Secretary-General addressed to the President of the Security Council

C.E.E. 06 Establishment of an International Tribunal for the Prosecution of Persons responsible for Serious Violations of International Humanitarian Law committed in the Territory of the Former Yugoslavia

Meetings: **1993**: **3175, 3217, 3265, 3296**
1994: **3401**
1996: **3637,** 3663
1997: **3763,** 3813
1998: 3878, **3919,** 3944
1999: **4033,** 4063
2000: 4150, 4161, 4229, **4240**

Resolution 808 (1993) of 22 February 1993
Resolution 827 (1993) of 25 May 1993
Resolution 857 (1993) of 20 August 1993
Resolution 877 (1993) of 21 October 1993
Resolution 963 (1994) of 8 July 1994
Resolution 1047 (1996) of 29 February 1996
Resolution 1104 (1997) of 8 April 1997
Resolution 1126 (1997) of 27 August 1997
Resolution 1166 (1998) of 13 May 1998
Resolution 1191 (1998) of 27 August 1998
Resolution 1207 (1998) of 17 November 1998

Resolution 1259 (1999) of 11 August 1999
Resolution 1329 (2000) of 30 November 2000

Statement, 8 May 1996

Letter dated 25 July 1994 from the President of the Security Council addressed to the Secretary-General

Letter dated 23 September 1994 from the President of the Security Council addressed to the Secretary-General

Letter dated 13 February 1996 from the Presidents of the International Criminal Tribunal for the Former Yugoslavia and Rwanda addressed to the President of the Security Council

Letter dated 24 April 1996 from the President of the International Tribunals for the Prosecution of Persons Responsible for Serious Violations of International Humanitarian Law committed in the Territory of the Former Yugoslavia since 1991 addressed to the President of the Security Council

Letter dated 22 May 1996 from the President of the International Tribunal for the Prosecution of Persons Responsible for Serious Violations of International Humanitarian Law committed in the Territory of the Former Yugoslavia since 1991 addressed to the President of the Security Council

Letter dated 27 June 1996 from the President of the Security Council addressed to the Presidents of the International Criminal Tribunals for the former Yugoslavia and Rwanda

Letter dated 11 July 1996 from the President of the International Tribunal for the Prosecution of Persons Responsible for Serious Violations of International Humanitarian Law commited in the territory of the former Yugoslavia since 1991 addressed to the President of the Security Council

Letter dated 16 September 1996 from the President of the International Tribunal for the Prosecution of Persons Responsible for Serious Violations of International Humanitarian Law committed in the territory of the former Yugoslavia since 1991 addressed to the President of the Security Council

Identical letters dated 30 July 1997 from the Secretary-General addressed to the President of the General Assembly and the President of the Security Council

Letter dated 8 September 1998 from the President of the International Tribunal for the Prosecution of Persons Responsible for Serious Violations of International Humanitarian Law committed in the territory of the former Yugoslavia since 1991 addressed to the President of the Security Council

Letter dated 6 November 1998 from the President of the International Tribunal for the Prosecution of Persons Responsible for Serious Violations of International Humanitarian Law committed in the territory of the former Yugoslavia since 1991 addressed to the President of the Security Council

Letter dated 25 November 1998 from the President of the International Tribunal for the Prosecution of Persons Responsible for Serious Violations of International Humanitarian Law committed in the territory of the former Yugoslavia since 1991 addressed to the President of the Security Council

Letter dated 16 March 1999 from the President of the International Tribunal for the Prosecution of Persons Responsible for Serious Violations of International Humanitarian Law committed in the territory of the former Yugoslavia since 1991 addressed to the President of the Security Council

Letter dated 6 April 1999 from the President of the International Tribunal for the Prosecution of Persons Responsible for Serious Violations of International Humanitarian Law committed in the territory of the former Yugoslavia since 1991 addressed to the President of the Security Council

Letter dated 9 June 1999 from the Secretary-General addressed to the President of the Security Council

Letter dated 21 June 1999 from the Secretary-General addressed to the President of the Security-Council

Letter dated 28 June 1999 from the President of the Security Council addressed to the Secretary-General

Letter dated 29 June 1999 from the Secretary-General addressed to the President of the Security Council

Letter dated 25 August 1999 from the President of the International Tribunal for the Prosecution of Persons Responsible for Serious Violations of International Humanitarian Law committed in the territory of the former Yugoslavia since 1991 addressed to the President of the Security Council

Identical letters dated 7 September 2000 from the Secretary-General addressed to the President of the General Assembly and the President of the Security Counsil.

Letter dated 26 September 2000 from the Secretary General addressed to the President of the Security Council

C.E.E. 07 Navigation on the Danube river in the Federal Republic of Yugoslavia (Serbia and Montenegro)

Meetings: **1993**: **3290**
1994: 3348
1995: **3533**

Resolution 992 (1995) of 11 May 1995

Statement, 28 January 1993
Statement, 10 February 1993
Statement, 13 October 1993
Statement, 14 March 1994

C.E.E. 08 Applications made under Article 50 of the Charter of the United Nations as a consequence of the implementation of measures imposed against the former Yugoslavia

Meetings: **1993**: **3240**

Resolution 843 (1993) of 18 June 1993

Letter dated 6 July 1993 from the President of the Security Council addressed to the Secretary-General

Letter dated 9 August 1993 from the President of the Security Council addressed to the Secretary-General

Letter dated 20 December 1993 from the President of the Security Council addressed to the Secretary-General

C.E.E. 09 Conference on Security and Cooperation in Europe (CSCE) in Kosovo, Sandzak and Vojvodina , the Federal Republic of Yugoslavia (Serbia and Montenegro)

Meetings: **1993: 3262**

Resolution 855 (1993) of 9 August 1993

C.E.E.10 The situation in the former Yugoslav Republic of Macedonia Reports of the Secretary-General on the United Nations Preventive Deployment Force (UNPREDEP)

Meetings: **1992: 3147**
1993: 3239
1995: 3602
1996: 3630, 3670, 3716
1997: 3764, 3783, 3836. 3839
1998: 3911
1999: 3982

Resolution 795 (1992) of 11 December 1992
Resolution 842 (1993) of 18 June 1993
Resolution 1027 (1995) of 30 November 1995
Resolution 1046 (1996) of 13 February 1996
Resolution 1058 (1996) of 30 May 1996
Resolution 1082 (1996) of 27 November 1996
Resolution 1105 (1997) of 9 April 1997

Resolution 1110 (1997) of 28 May 1997
Resolution 1140 (1997) of 28 November 1997
Resolution 1142 (1997) of 4 December 1997
Resolution 1186 (1998) of 21 July 1998

Letter dated 23 November 1992 from the Secretary-General addressed to the President of the Security Council

Letter dated 25 November 1992 from the President of the Security Council addressed to the Secretary-General

Letter dated 22 July 1993 from the President of the Security Council addressed to the Secretary-General

Letter dated 1 February 1996 from the President of the Security Council addressed to the Secretary-General

Letter dated 6 February 1996 from the Secretary-General addressed to the President of the Security Council

Letter dated 3 April 1997 from the Secretary-General addressed to the President of the Security Council

C.E.E. 11 Membership of the Former Yugoslav Republic of Macedonia
Interim accord between Greece and the former Yugoslav Republic of Macedonia

Meetings: **1993**: **3243**
1995: 3579

Resolution 845 (1993) of 18 June 1993

Statement, 15 September 1995

Letter dated 11 April 1994 from the President of the Security Council addressed to the Secretary-General

Letter dated 7 June 1994 from the President of the Security Council addressed to the Secretary-General

Letter dated 17 August 1994 from the President of the Security Council addressed to the Secretary-General

C.E.E. 12 Membership of the United Nations and participation in UN activities by the Federal Republic of Yugoslavia (Serbia and Montenegro)

Meetings: **1992**: **3116**
1993: **3204**

Resolution 777 (1992) of 19 September 1992
Resolution 821 (1993) of 28 April 1993

Letter dated 9 December 1992 from the President of the Security Council addressed to the President of the General Assembly

Letter dated 17 September 1993 from the President of the Security Council addressed to the President of the General Assembly

Letter dated 11 April 1994 from the President of the Security Council addressed to the Secretary-General

Letter dated 7 June 1994 from the President of the Security Council addressed to the Secretary-General

Letter dated 17 August 1994 from the President of the Security Council addressed to the Secretary-General

C.E.E. 13 The Situation in Albania

Meetings: **1997**: 3751, **3758, 3791,** 3811, 3812

Resolution 1101 (1997) of 28 March 1997
Resolution 1114 (1997) of 19 June 1997

Statement, 13 March 1997
Statement, 14 August 1997

C.E.E.14 The Federal Republic of Yugoslavia (Serbia and Montenegro)
The situation in Kosovo
Security Council Resolutions 1160 (1998), 1199 (1998) and 1203 (1998), 1239 (1999) and 1244 (1999)
Report of the Security Council Mission on the implementation of Security Council resolution 1244 (1999)
Report of the Secretary-General on the UN Interim Administration in Kosovo (UNMIK)

Meetings: **1998**: **3868,** 3918, **3930, 3937**
1999: 3967, 3974, 3988, 3989, 4000, 4001, **4003, 4011,** 4011 (Resumption 1), **4061, 4086**
2000: 4102, 4108, 4138, 4153, 4171, 4190, 4200, 4225, 4232, 4249, 4250

Resolution 1160 (1998) of 31 March 1998
Resolution 1199 (1998) of 23 September 1998
Resolution 1203 (1998) of 24 October 1998
Resolution 1239 (1999) of 14 May 1999
Resolution 1244 (1999) of 10 June 1999

Statement, 24 August 1998
Statement, 19 January 1999
Statement, 29 January 1999
Statement, 14 May 1999
Statement, 22 November 2000
Statement, 19 December 2000

Letter dated 8 April 1998 from the Secretary-General addressed to the President of the Security Council

Letter dated 14 October 1998 from the Secretary-General addressed to the President of the Security Council

Letter dated 19 October 1998 from the President of the Security Council addressed to the Secretary-General

Letter dated 18 December 1998 from the Secretary-General addressed to the President of the Security Council

Letter dated 18 June 1999 from the Secretary-General addressed to the President of the Security Council

Letter dated 21 June 1999 from the Secretary-General addressed to the President of the Security Council

Letter dated 18 November 1999 the Secretary-General addressed to the President of the Security Council

Letter dated 14 April 2000 from the President of the Security Council addressed to the Security General.

4

AFRICA

AF. 01 Complaint by Lebanon

Meetings: **1958**: 818, 822, 823, 824, **825,** 827, 828, 829, 830, 831, 832, 833, 834, 835, 836, 837, **838.**

Resolution 128 (1958) of 11 June 1958
Resolution 129 (1958) of 7 August 1958

AF. 02 The Congo question

Meetings: **1960**: **873,** 877, 878, **879,** 884, 885, **886,** 887, 888, 889, 896, 897, 899, 900, 901, 902, 903, 904, 905, **906,** 912, **913, 914, 915, 916, 917, 918, 919, 920.**
1961: 924, 925, 926, 927, 928, 929, 930, 931, 932, 933, 934, 935, 936, 937, 938, 939, 940, 941, **942,** 973, 974, 975, 976, 977, 978, 979, **982.**

Resolution 143 (1960) of 14 July 1960
Resolution 145 (1960) of 22 July 1960
Resolution 146 (1960) of 9 August 1960
Resolution 157 (1960) of 17 September 1960
Resolution 161 (1961) of 21 February 1961
Resolution 169 (1961) of 24 November 1961

K. Wellens (ed.),
Resolutions and Statements of the United Nations Security Council (1946-2000), 31–73.

AF. 03 Complaint by Tunisia (July 1961)

Meetings: **1961**: 961, **962,** 963, 964, 965, 966.

Resolution 164 (1961) of 22 July 1961

AF. 04 Questions concerning the Democratic Republic of the Congo

Meetings: **1964**: 1170, 1171, 1172, 1173, 1174, 1175, 1176, 1177, 1178, 1181, 1183, 1184, 1185, 1186, 1187, 1188, **1189.**
1966: 1302, 1303, 1304, **1306.**
1967: 1363, 1364, **1367,** 1372, 1374, 1376, **1378.**

Resolution 199 (1964) of 30 December 1964
Resolution 226 (1966) of 14 October 1966
Resolution 239 (1967) of 10 July 1967
Resolution 241 (1967) of 15 November 1967

AF. 05 Consideration of questions relating to Africa of which the Security Council is currently seized and implementation of the Council's relevant resolutions

Meetings: **1972**: 1624, 1625, **1626,** 1627, 1628, 1629, 1630, 1631, 1632, 1633, 1634, 1635, 1636, 1637, 1638, 1639.

Resolution 308 (1972) of 19 January 1972

Statement, 4 February 1972

AF. 06 The Situation concerning Western Sahara

Meetings: **1975**: 1849, **1850, 1852,** 1853, **1854.**
1988: **2826.**
1990: **2929.**
1991: 2984, 3025.

1993: **3179**.
1994: **3355**, 3411, 3457
1995: **3490**, 3516, **3540**, **3550**, **3582**, **3610**
1996: **3625**, **3668**, **3718**
1997: 3754, **3779**, **3821**, **3825**
1998: **3849**, **3873**, **3910**, **3929**, **3938**, 3956
1999: **3971**, **3976**, **3990**, **3994**, **4002**, **4044**, **4080**
2000: **4106**, **4149**, **4175**, 4210, **4211**

Resolution 377 (1975) of 22 October 1975
Resolution 379 (1975) of 2 November 1975
Resolution 380 (1975) of 6 November 1975
Resolution 621 (1988) of 20 September 1988
Resolution 658 (1990) of 27 June 1990
Resolution 690 (1991) of 29 April 1991
Resolution 725 (1991) of 31 December 1991
Resolution 809 (1993) of 2 March 1993
Resolution 907 (1994) of 29 March 1994
Resolution 973 (1995) of 13 January 1995
Resolution 995 (1995) of 26 May 1995
Resolution 1002 (1995) of 30 June 1995
Resolution 1017 (1995) of 22 September 1995
Resolution 1033 (1995) of 19 December 1995
Resolution 1042 (1996) of 31 January 1996
Resolution 1056 (1996) of 29 June 1996
Resolution 1084 (1996) of 27 November 1996
Resolution 1108 (1997) of 22 May 1997
Resolution 1131 (1997) of 29 September 1997
Resolution 1133 (1997) of 20 October 1997
Resolution 1148 (1998) of 26 January 1998
Resolution 1163 (1998) of 17 April 1998
Resolution 1185 (1998) of 20 July 1998
Resolution 1198 (1998) of 18 September 1998
Resolution 1204 (1998) of 30 October 1998
Resolution 1215 (1999) of 17 December 1998
Resolution 1224 (1999) of 28 January 1999
Resolution 1228 (1999) of 11 February 1999
Resolution 1232 (1999) of 30 March 1999

Resolution 1235 (1999) of 30 April 1999
Resolution 1238 (1999) of 14 May 1999
Resolution 1263 (1999) of 13 September 1999
Resolution 1282 (1999) of 14 December 1999
Resolution 1292 (2000) of 29 February 2000
Resolution 1301 (2000) of 31 May 2000
Resolution 1309 (2000) of 25 July 2000
Resolution 1324 (2000) of 30 October 2000

Statement, 29 July 1994
Statement, 15 November 1994
Statement, 12 April 1995
Statement, 19 March 1997

Presidential Appeal, 6 November 1975

Letter dated 3 June 1992 from the President of the Security Council addressed to the Secretary-General

Letter dated 31 August 1992 from the President of the Security Council addressed to the Secretary-General

Letter dated 8 October 1992 from the President of the Security Council addressed to the Secretary-General

Letter dated 28 May 1993 from the President of the Security Council addressed to the Secretary-General

Letter dated 4 August 1993 from the President of the Security Council addressed to the Secretary-General

Letter dated 6 December 1993 from the President of the Security Council addressed to the Secretary-General

Letter dated 17 March 1997 from the Secretary-General addressed to the President of the Security Council

Letter dated 12 September 1997 from the Secretary-General addressed to the President of the Security Council

Letter dated 12 December 1997 from the Secretary-General addressed to the President of the Security Council

Letter dated 19 February 1998 from the Secretary-General addressed to the President of the Security Council

AF. 07 Complaint by Benin

Meetings: **1977**: 1986, 1987, 2000, 2001, 2002, 2003, 2004, **2005**, 2047, 2048, **2049.**

Resolution 404 (1977) of 8 February 1977
Resolution 405 (1977) of 14 April 1977
Resolution 419 (1977) of 24 November 1977

AF. 08 Letter dated 31 March 1982 from the President of the Republic of Kenya to the President of the Security Council enclosing the letter dated 18 March 1982 from the President of the Republic of Chad to the President of the Security Council

Meetings: **1982**: **2358.**

Resolution 504 (1982) of 30 April 1982

AF. 09 Complaint by Tunisia against Israel

Meetings: **1985**: 2610, 2611, 2613, **2615.**

Resolution 573 (1985) of 4 October 1985

AF. 10 Question relating to Angola (May 1961)

Meetings: **1961**: 943, 944, 945, 946, 950, 951, 952, 953, 954, 955, **956.**

Resolution 163 (1961) of 9 June 1961

AF. 11 Complaint by Senegal against Portugal

Meetings: **1963**: 1027, 1028, 1029, 1030, 1031, 1032, **1033.**
1965: 1205, 1206, 1210, 1211, **1212.**
1969: 1516, 1517, 1518, 1519, **1520.**
1971: 1569, 1570, 1571, **1572,** 1586, 1599, 1600, **1601.**
1972: 1667, 1668, **1669.**

Resolution 178 (1963) of 24 April 1963
Resolution 204 (1965) of 19 May 1965
Resolution 273 (1969) of 9 December 1969
Resolution 294 (1971) of 15 July 1971
Resolution 302 (1971) of 24 November 1971
Resolution 321 (1972) of 23 October 1972

AF. 12 Question relating to territories under Portuguese administration
Question concerning the situation in territories under Portuguese administration

Meetings: **1963**: 1040, 1041, 1042, 1043, 1044, 1045, 1046, 1047, 1048, **1049,** 1079, 1080, 1081, 1082, **1083.**
1965: 1250, 1253, 1254, 1255, 1256, 1266, 1267, **1268.**
1972: **1639,** 1672, 1673, 1674, 1675, 1676, **1677.**

Resolution 180 (1963) of 31 July 1963
Resolution 183 (1963) of 11 December 1963
Resolution 218 (1965) of 23 November 1965
Resolution 312 (1972) of 4 February 1972
Resolution 322 (1972) of 22 November 1972

AF. 13 Complaint by Guinea against Portugal

Meetings: **1969**: 1522, 1523, 1524, 1525, **1526.**
1970: **1558,** 1559, 1560, 1561, 1562, **1563.**
1971: **1573,** 1576, 1586, 1603.

Resolution 275 (1969) of 22 December 1969
Resolution 289 (1970) of 23 November 1970
Resolution 290 (1970) of 8 December 1970
Resolution 295 (1971) of 3 August 1971

Statement, 26 August 1971
Statement, 30 November 1971

AF. 14 Question concerning the situation in Southern Rhodesia

Meetings: **1963**: **1064.**
1965: 1194, 1195, 1197, 1199, 1201, **1202,** 1257, **1258,** 1259, 1260, 1261, 1262, 1263, 1264, **1265.**
1966: 1276, **1277,** 1278, 1279, 1280, 1281, 1282, 1283, 1284, 1285, 1331, 1332, 1333, 1335, 1336, 1337, 1338, 1339, **1340.**
1968: 1399, 1400, 1408, 1413, 1415, **1428.**
1970: 1530, 1531, 1532, 1533, 1534, **1535,** 1556, **1557.**
1971: 1603, 1609.
1972: 1640, 1641, 1642, **1645,** 1654, **1655,** 1663, 1664, 1665, **1666.**
1973: 1712, 1713, 1714, 1715, **1716.**
1976: 1890, 1891, 1892, **1907.**
1977: **2011,** 2033, **2034.**
1978: 2061, 2062, 2063, 2064, 2065, 2066, **2067, 2090.**
1979: 2119, 2120, 2121, **2122,** 2142, **2143, 2181.**
1980: 2192, 2193, 2194, 2195, **2196.**

Resolution 202 (1965) of 6 May 1965
Resolution 216 (1965) of 12 November 1965
Resolution 217 (1965) of 20 November 1965

Resolution 221 (1966) of 9 April 1966
Resolution 232 (1966) of 16 December 1966
Resolution 253 (1968) of 29 May 1968
Resolution 277 (1970) of 18 March 1970
Resolution 288 (1970) of 17 November 1970
Resolution 314 (1972) of 28 February 1972
Resolution 318 (1972) of 28 July 1972
Resolution 320 (1972) of 29 September 1972
Resolution 333 (1973) of 22 May 1973
Resolution 388 (1976) of 6 April 1976
Resolution 409 (1977) of 27 May 1977
Resolution 415 (1977) of 29 September 1977
Resolution 423 (1978) of 14 March 1978
Resolution 437 (1978) of 10 October 1978
Resolution 445 (1979) of 8 March 1979
Resolution 448 (1979) of 30 April 1979
Resolution 460 (1979) of 21 December 1979
Resolution 463 (1980) of 2 February 1980

AF. 15 Request by Mozambique under Article 50 of the Charter of the United Nations in relation to the situation which has arisen as a result of its decision to impose sanctions against Southern Rhodesia in full implementation of the relevant decisions of the Security Council

Meetings: **1976**: 1890, 1891, **1892.**

Resolution 386 (1976) of 17 March 1976

AF. 16 Complaint by Mozambique against the illegal régime in Southern Rhodesia

Meetings: **1977**: 2014, 2015, 2016, 2017, 2018, **2019.**

Resolution 411 (1977) of 30 June 1977

AF. 17 Complaint of the Government of Botswana against the illegal régime in Southern Rhodesia concerning violations of its territorial sovereignty as contained in the letter dated 22 December 1976 from the Permanent Representative of Botswana to the United Nations addressed to the President of the Security Council

Meetings: **1977**: 1983, 1984, **1985**, 2006, **2008.**

Resolution 403 (1977) of 14 January 1977
Resolution 406 (1977) of 25 May 1977

AF. 18 Complaint by Zambia against Portugal

Meetings: **1969**: 1486, 1487, 1488, 1489, 1490, **1491.**

Resolution 268 (1969) of 28 July 1969

AF. 19 Complaint by Zambia against South Africa

Meetings: **1971**: 1590, 1591, **1592.**
1976: 1944, 1945, 1946, 1947, **1948.**
1980: 2209, 2210, **2211.**

Resolution 300 (1971) of 12 October 1971
Resolution 393 (1976) of 30 July 1976
Resolution 466 (1980) of 11 April 1980

AF. 20 Complaint by Zambia against Southern Rhodesia

Meetings: **1973**: 1687, 1688, 1689, **1690,** 1691, 1692, 1693, **1694.**
1978: 2068, 2069, **2070.**
1979: **2171.**

Resolution 326 (1973) of 2 February 1973
Resolution 327 (1973) of 2 February 1973

Resolution 328 (1973) of 10 March 1973
Resolution 329 (1973) of 10 March 1973
Resolution 424 (1978) of 17 March 1978
Resolution 455 (1979) of 23 November 1979

AF. 21 Complaint by Kenya on behalf of the African Group of States at the United Nations, concerning the act of aggression committed by South Africa against the People's Republic of Angola

Meetings: **1976**: 1900, 1901, 1902, 1903, 1904, 1905, **1906.**

Resolution 387 (1976) of 31 March 1976

AF. 22 Complaint by Lesotho against South Africa

Meetings: **1976**: 1981, **1982.**
1977: 2007, **2009.**
1982: 2406, **2407,** 2408, 2409.
1983: **2455.**
1985: 2638, **2639.**

Resolution 402 (1976) of 22 December 1976
Resolution 407 (1977) of 25 May 1977
Resolution 527 (1982) of 15 December 1982
Resolution 535 (1983) of 29 June 1983
Resolution 580 (1985) of 30 December 1985

AF. 23 Complaint by Angola against South Africa

Meetings: **1978**: 2077, **2078.**
1979: 2130, 2132, 2133, 2135, 2136, 2137, 2138, **2139,** 2169, **2170.**
1980: 2237, **2240.**
1983: 2504, 2505, 2506, 2507, **2508.**
1984: 2509, 2510, **2511.**

1985: 2596, **2597,** 2606, **2607,** 2612, 2614, 2616, **2617, 2631.**
1987: 2763, 2764, 2765, 2766, **2767, 2778.**

Resolution 428 (1978) of 6 May 1978
Resolution 447 (1979) of 28 March 1979
Resolution 454 (1979) of 2 November 1979
Resolution 475 (1980) of 27 June 1980
Resolution 545 (1983) of 20 December 1983
Resolution 546 (1984) of 6 January 1984
Resolution 567 (1985) of 20 June 1985
Resolution 571 (1985) of 20 September 1985
Resolution 574 (1985) of 7 October 1985
Resolution 577 (1985) of 6 December 1985
Resolution 602 (1987) of 25 November 1987
Resolution 606 (1987) of 23 December 1987

AF. 24 Complaint by Botswana against South Africa

Meetings: **1985**: 2598, **2599, 2609.**

Resolution 568 (1985) of 21 June 1985
Resolution 572 (1985) of 30 September 1985

Statement, 24 June 1988

AF. 25 The situation in Southern Africa

Meetings: **1986**: 2652, 2654, 2656, 2657, 2658, 2659, 2660, 2661, **2662,** 2684, 2685, 2686.

Resolution 581 (1986) of 13 February 1986

AF. 26 Question relating to the situation in the Union of South Africa

Meetings: **1960**: 851, 852, 853, 854, 855, **856.**

Resolution 134 (1960) of 1 April 1960

AF. 27 Question relating to the policies of apartheid of the Government of the Republic of South Africa

Meetings: **1963**: 1040, 1050, 1051, 1052, 1053, 1054, 1055, **1056,** 1073, 1074, 1075, 1076, 1077, **1078.**
1964: 1127, **1128,** 1129, 1130, 1131, 1132, 1133, 1134, **1135.**

Resolution 181 (1963) of 7 August 1963
Resolution 182 (1963) of 4 December 1963
Resolution 190 (1964) of 9 June 1964
Resolution 191 (1964) of 18 June 1964

AF. 28 The question of race conflict in South Africa resulting from the policies of apartheid of the Government of the Republic of South Africa

Meetings: **1970**: 1545, 1546, 1547, 1548, **1549.**
1972: **1639.**

Resolution 282 (1970) of 23 July 1970
Resolution 311 (1972) of 4 February 1972

AF. 29 Situation in South Africa: killings and violence by the apartheid - régime in South Africa in Soweto and other areas

Meetings: **1976**: 1929, **1930.**

Resolution 392 (1976) of 19 June 1976

AF. 30 The Question of South Africa

Meetings: **1977**: 1988, 1989, 1990, 1991, 1992, 1994, 1996, 1998, 1999, 2036, 2037, 2038, 2039, 2040, 2042, 2043, 2044, **2045, 2046, 2052,** 2053.
1980: 2225, 2227, 2228, 2229, **2231,** 2261.
1982: **2351,** 2397, 2398, **2404.**
1983: **2452.**
1984: **2512,** 2548, 2549, 2550, **2551, 2560, 2564.**
1985: 2571, **2574,** 2600, 2601, **2602,** 2603, 2623.
1986: 2690, **2723.**
1987: 2732, 2733, 2734, 2735, 2736, 2737, 2738.
1988: 2793, 2794, 2795, 2796, 2797, **2799, 2817, 2830.**
1992: 3095, **3096, 3107.**
1993: 3197, 3267, 3318.
1994: **3329,** 3365, **3379, 3393.**

Resolution 417 (1977) of 31 October 1977
Resolution 418 (1977) of 4 November 1977
Resolution 421 (1977) of 9 December 1977
Resolution 473 (1980) of 13 June 1980
Resolution 503 (1982) of 9 April 1982
Resolution 525 (1982) of 7 December 1982
Resolution 533 (1983) of 7 June 1983
Resolution 547 (1984) of 13 January 1984
Resolution 554 (1984) of 17 August 1984
Resolution 556 (1984) of 23 October 1984
Resolution 558 (1984) of 13 December 1984
Resolution 560 (1985) of 12 March 1985
Resolution 569 (1985) of 26 July 1985
Resolution 591 (1986) of 28 November 1986
Resolution 610 (1988) of 16 March 1988
Resolution 615 (1988) of 17 June 1988
Resolution 623 (1988) of 23 November 1988
Resolution 765 (1992) of 16 July 1992
Resolution 772 (1992) of 17 August 1992
Resolution 894 (1994) of 14 January 1994
Resolution 919 (1994) of 25 May 1994

Resolution 930 (1994) of 27 June 1994

Statement, 5 April 1979
Statement, 21 September 1979
Statement, 5 February 1981
Statement, 15 December 1981
Statement, 4 October 1982
Statement, 20 August 1985
Statement, 21 August 1985
Statement, 17 October 1985
Statement, 13 June 1986
Statement, 16 April 1987
Statement, 17 August 1992
Statement, 10 September 1992
Statement, 12 April 1993
Statement, 24 August 1993
Statement, 23 November 1993
Statement, 19 April 1994

Letter dated 19 February 1993 from the President of the Security Council to the Secretary-General

AF. 31 The question of South West Africa
The situation in Namibia

Meetings: **1968**: **1387,** 1390, 1391, 1392, 1393, 1394, 1395, 1396, **1397.**
1969: 1464, **1465,** 1492, 1493, 1494, 1495, 1496, **1497.**
1970: 1527, 1528, **1529, 1550.**
1971: 1583, 1584, 1585, 1587, 1588, 1589, 1593, 1594, 1595, 1597, **1598.**
1972: **1638,** 1656, **1657,** 1678, 1679, 1680, 1681, **1682.**
1973: 1684, 1756, 1757, **1758.**
1974: **1811,** 1812.
1976: 1880, 1881, 1882, 1883, 1884, **1885,** 1954, 1956, 1957, 1958, 1959, 1960, 1961, 1962, 1963.
1978: **2082, 2087,** 2088, 2092, 2094, 2095, 2096, 2097, **2098,** 2103, 2104.

1983: 2439, 2440, 2441, 2442, 2443, 2444, 2446, 2447, 2448, **2449**, 2450, 2451, 2481, 2482, 2483, 2484, 2485, 2486, 2488, 2490, **2492.**

1985: 2583, 2584, 2585, 2586, 2587, 2588, 2589, 2590, 2592, 2593, 2594, **2595**, 2624, 2625, 2626, 2628, 2629.

1987: 2740, 2741, 2742, 2743, 2744, 2745, 2746, 2747, 2755, 2756, 2757, 2758, **2759.**

1988: 2827.

1989: **2842, 2848**, 2876, 2877, 2878, 2879, 2880, 2881, **2882, 2886**, 2893.

Resolution 245 (1968) of 25 January 1968
Resolution 246 (1968) of 14 March 1968
Resolution 264 (1969) of 20 March 1969
Resolution 269 (1969) of 12 August 1969
Resolution 276 (1970) of 30 January 1970
Resolution 283 (1970) of 29 July 1970
Resolution 284 (1970) of 29 July 1970
Resolution 301 (1971) of 20 October 1971
Resolution 309 (1972) of 4 February 1972
Resolution 310 (1972) of 4 February 1972
Resolution 319 (1972) of 1 August 1972
Resolution 323 (1972) of 6 December 1972
Resolution 342 (1973) of 11 December 1973
Resolution 366 (1974) of 17 December 1974
Resolution 385 (1976) of 30 January 1976
Resolution 431 (1978) of 27 July 1978
Resolution 432 (1978) of 27 July 1978
Resolution 435 (1978) of 29 September 1978
Resolution 439 (1978) of 13 November 1978
Resolution 532 (1983) of 31 May 1983
Resolution 539 (1983) of 28 October 1983
Resolution 566 (1985) of 19 June 1985
Resolution 601 (1987) of 30 October 1987
Resolution 628 (1989) of 16 January 1989
Resolution 629 (1989) of 16 January 1989
Resolution 632 (1989) of 16 February 1989
Resolution 640 (1989) of 29 August 1989

Resolution 643 (1989) of 31 October 1989

Statement, 28 November 1979
Statement, 3 May 1985
Statement, 21 August 1987
Statement, 29 September 1988
Statement, 3 November 1989
Statement, 20 November 1989

AF. 32 Complaint by Tunisia against Israel

Meetings: **1988**: 2807, 2808, 2809, **2810**

Resolution 611 (1988) of 25 April 1988

AF. 33 The situation in Angola (UNAVEM I)

Meetings: **1988**: **2834.**

Resolution 626 (1988) of 20 December 1988

AF. 34 The situation in Angola (UNAVEM II)

Meetings: **1991**: **2991**
1992: **3062**
1992: 3092, 3115, 3120, 3126, **3130, 3144,** 3152
1993: **3168, 3182, 3206, 3226,** 3232, **3254, 3277,** 3302, **3323**
1994: 3335, **3350, 3384, 3395,** 3417, 3423, **3431, 3445,** 3450, **3477**

Resolution 696 (1991) of 30 May 1991
Resolution 747 (1992) of 24 March 1992
Resolution 785 (1992) of 30 December 1992
Resolution 793 (1992) of 30 November 1992
Resolution 804 (1993) of 29 January 1993
Resolution 811 (1993) of 12 March 1993

Resolution 823 (1993) of 30 April 1993
Resolution 834 (1993) of 1 June 1993
Resolution 851 (1993) of 15 July 1993
Resolution 864 (1993) of 15 September 1993
Resolution 890 (1993) of 15 December 1993
Resolution 903 (1994) of 16 March 1994
Resolution 922 (1994) of 31 May 1994
Resolution 932 (1994) of 30 June 1994
Resolution 945 (1994) of 29 September 1994
Resolution 952 (1994) of 27 October 1994
Resolution 966 (1994) of 8 December 1994

Statement, 7 July 1992
Statement, 18 September 1992
Statement, 6 October 1992
Statement, 19 October 1992
Statement, 27 October 1992
Statement, 2 December 1992
Statement, 22 December 1992
Statement, 9 June 1993
Statement, 1 November 1993
Statement, 10 February 1994
Statement, 12 August 1994
Statement, 9 September 1994
Statement, 4 November 1994

Note dated 8 October 1992 issued by the President of the Security Council

Letter dated 14 April 1994 from the Security Council addressed to the Secretary-General

Note dated 18 February 1999 issued by the President of the Security Council

AF. 35 The Lockerbie disaster

Meetings: **1992**: **3033, 3063,** 3064.
1993: **3312**

1996: 3655
1997: 3734, 3761, 3777
1998: 3864, **3920**
1999: **3992,** 4022

Resolution 731 (1992) of 21 January 1992
Resolution 748 (1992) of 31 March 1992
Resolution 883 (1993) of 11 November 1993
Resolution 1192 (1998) of 27 August 1998

Statement, 2 April 1992
Statement, 12 August 1992
Statement, 9 December 1992
Statement, 8 April 1993
Statement, 13 August 1993
Statement, 10 December 1993
Statement, 8 April 1994
Statement, 5 August 1994
Statement, 30 November 1994
Statement, 30 March 1995
Statement, 28 July 1995
Statement, 22 November 1995
Statement, 18 April 1996
Statement, 29 January 1997
Statement, 4 April 1997
Statement, 20 May 1997
Statement, 8 April 1999
Statement, 9 July 1999

Letter dated 18 December 1997 from the Secretary-General addressed to the President of the Security Council

Letter dated 5 April 1999 from the Secretary-General addressed to the President of the Security Council

Letter dated 25 April 2000 from the Secretary-General addressed to the President of the Security Council

AF. 36 The Situation in Somalia

Meetings: **1992**: **3039, 3060, 3069, 3101, 3110, 3145**
1993: **3188, 3229, 3282, 3315, 3317**
1994: **3334, 3385,** 3418, **3432, 3446, 3447**
1995: 3513
1996: 3620, 3641, 3726
1997: 3742, 3770, 3845
1999: 4010, 4066
2000: 4166, 4167, 4196

Resolution 733 (1992) of 23 January 1992
Resolution 746 (1992) of 17 March 1992
Resolution 751 (1992) of 24 April 1992
Resolution 767 (1992) of 27 July 1992
Resolution 775 (1992) of 28 August 1992
Resolution 794 (1992) of 3 December 1992
Resolution 814 (1993) of 26 March 1993
Resolution 837 (1993) of 6 June 1993
Resolution 865 (1993) of 22 September 1993
Resolution 878 (1993) of 29 October 1993
Resolution 885 (1993) of 16 November 1993
Resolution 886 (1993) of 18 November 1993
Resolution 897 (1994) of 4 February 1994
Resolution 923 (1994) of 31 May 1994
Resolution 946 (1994) of 30 September 1994
Resolution 953 (1994) of 31 October 1994
Resolution 954 (1994) of 4 November 1994

Statement, 16 October 1992
Statement, 25 August 1994
Statement, 6 April 1995
Statement, 24 January 1996
Statement, 20 December 1996
Statement, 27 February 1997
Statement, 23 December 1997
Statement, 27 May 1999

Statement, 12 November 1999
Statement, 29 June 2000

Letter dated 27 August 1993 from the President of the Security Council addressed to the Secretary-General

Letter dated 1 October 1993 from the President of the Security Council addressed to the Secretary-General

Letter dated 26 May 1994 from the President of the Security Council addressed to the Secretary-General

Letter dated 28 July 1994 from the President of the Security Council addressed to the Secretary-General

Letter dated 7 December 1994 from the President of the Security Council addressed to the Secretary-General

Letter dated 11 April 1996 from the Secretary-General addressed to the President of the Security Council

Letter dated 2 November 1999 from the Secretary-General addressed to the President of the Security Council

Letter dated 5 November 1999 from the President of the Security Council addressed to the Secretary-General

AF. 37 The Situation in Mozambique: Reports of the Secretary-General on the United Nations Operation in Mozambique (ONUMUZ)

Meetings: **1992**: 3125, **3149, 3123**
1993: **3198, 3253, 3274, 3300, 3305**
1994: **3338, 3444, 3375,** 3406, 3422, **3458, 3464,** 3479
1995: 3494

Resolution 782 (1992) of 13 October 1992
Resolution 797 (1992) of 16 December 1992

Resolution 818 (1993) of 14 April 1993
Resolution 850 (1993) of 9 July 1993
Resolution 863 (1993) of 13 September 1993
Resolution 879 (1993) of 29 October 1993
Resolution 882 (1993) of 5 November 1993
Resolution 898 (1993) of 23 February 1994
Resolution 916 (1994) of 5 May 1994
Resolution 957 (1994) of 15 November 1994
Resolution 960 (1994) of 21 November 1994

Statement, 27 October 1992
Statement, 19 July 1994
Statement, 7 September 1994
Statement, 21 October 1994
Statement, 14 December 1994

Letter dated 21 April 1994 from the President of the Security Council addressed to the Secretary-General

Note dated 4 August 1994 from the President of the Security Council addressed to the Secretary-General

AF. 38 The Situation in Liberia
Reports of the Secretary-General on the United Nations Observer Mission in Liberia (UNOMIL)

Meetings: **1992**: 3071, **3138**
1993: **3187,** 3233, **3263,** 3281
1994: 3339, **3366,** 3378, 3424, **3442,** 3404
1995: **3489, 3517, 3549, 3577, 3592**
1996: 3621, **3624,** 3649, 3661, 3667, **3671, 3694, 3717**
1997: **3757, 3793,** 3805

Resolution 788 (1992) of 19 November 1992
Resolution 813 (1993) of 26 March 1993
Resolution 856 (1993) of 10 August 1993
Resolution 866 (1993) of 22 September 1993

Resolution 911 (1994) of 21 April 1994
Resolution 950 (1994) of 21 October 1994
Resolution 972 (1995) of 13 January 1995
Resolution 985 (1995) of 13 April 1995
Resolution 1001 (1995) of 30 June 1995
Resolution 1014 (1995) of 15 September 1995
Resolution 1020 (1995) of 10 November 1995
Resolution 1041 (1995) of 29 January 1996
Resolution 1059 (1996) of 31 May 1996
Resolution 1071 (1996) of 30 August 1996
Resolution 1083 (1996) of 27 November 1996
Resolution 1100 (1997) of 27 March 1997
Resolution 1116 (1997) of 27 June 1997

Statement, 22 January 1991
Statement, 7 May 1992
Statement, 9 June 1993
Statement, 25 February 1994
Statement, 23 May 1994
Statement, 13 July 1994
Statement, 13 September 1994
Statement, 9 April 1996
Statement, 6 May 1996
Statement, 30 July 1997

Letter dated 16 December 1993 from the President of the Security Council addressed to the Secretary-General

Letter dated 18 January 1994 from the President of the Security Council addressed to the Secretary-General

Letter dated 19 April 1996 from the Secretary-General addressed to the President of the Security-Council

Letter dated 8 November 1996 from the President of the Security Council addressed to the Secretary-General

Letter dated 25 February 1997 from the Secretary-General addressed to the President of the Security Council

Letter dated 24 July 1997 from the Secretary-General addressed to the President of the Security Council

Letter dated 22 October 1997 from the Secretary-General addressed to the President of the Security Council

Letter dated 11 November 1998 from the Secretary-General addressed to the President of the Security Council

Letter dated 16 November 1998 from the President of the Security Council addressed to the Secretary-General

Letter dated 28 September 2000 from the Secretary-General addressed to the President of the Security Council

Letter dated 3 October 2000 from the President of the Security Council addressed to the Secretary-General

AF. 39 Agreement signed on 4 April 1994 between the Governments of Chad and the Libyan Arab Jamahiriya concerning the practical modalities for the implementation of the Judgment delivered by the International Court of Justice on 3 February 1994!

Meetings: **1994: 3363, 3373, 3389**

Resolution 910 (1994) of 14 April 1994
Resolution 915 (1994) of 4 May 1994
Resolution 926 (1994) of 13 June 1994

AF. 40 Letter dated 9 January 1996 from the Permanent Representative of Ethiopia to the United Nations addressed to the President of the Security Council concerning the extradition of the suspects wanted in the assassination attempt on the life of the President of the Arab Republic of Egypt in Addis Ababa, Ethiopia on 26 June 1995

Meetings: **1996**: **3627, 3660, 3690**

Resolution 1044 (1996) of 31 January 1996
Resolution 1054 (1996) of 26 April 1996
Resolution 1070 (1996) of 16 August 1996

AF. 41 Signature of the African Nuclear-Weapons-Free Zone Treaty (The Treaty of Pelindaba)

Meetings: **1996**: 3651

Statement, 12 April 1996

AF. 42 The Situation in Angola (UNAVEM III)

Meetings: **1994**: 3463
1995: **3499,** 3508, 3518, 3534, **3562,** 3586, 3598, 3614
1996: **3629,** 3657, **3662, 3679,** 3702, **3703, 3722**
1997: 3736, **3743,** 3755, **3759,** 3767, **3769, 3795,** 3803, **3820**
1998: 3884

Resolution 976 (1995) of 8 February 1995
Resolution 1008 (1995) of 7 August 1995
Resolution 1045 (1996) of 8 February 1996
Resolution 1055 (1996) of 8 April 1996
Resolution 1064 (1996) of 11 July 1996
Resolution 1075 (1996) of 11 October 1996
Resolution 1087 (1996) of 11 December 1996
Resolution 1098 (1997) of 27 February 1997
Resolution 1102 (1997) of 31 March 1997
Resolution 1106 (1997) of 16 April 1997
Resolution 1118 (1997) of 30 June 1997
Resolution 1130 (1997) of 29 September 1997

Statement, 21 November 1994
Statement, 10 March 1995
Statement, 13 April 1995
Statement, 11 May 1995
Statement, 12 October 1995
Statement, 28 November 1995
Statement, 21 December 1995
Statement, 24 April 1996
Statement, 30 January 1997
Statement, 21 March 1997
Statement, 23 July 1997
Statement, 22 May 1998

Letter dated 15 January 1996 from the President of the Security Council addressed to the President of the Republic of Angola

Letter dated 15 January 1996 from the President of the Security Council addressed to the President of the National Union for the Total Independence of Angola

Letter dated 22 May 1996 from the President of the Security Council addressed to the President of the Republic of Angola

Letter dated 22 May 1996 from the President of the Security Council addressed to the President of the National Union for the Total Independence of Angola

AF. 43 The Situation in Angola
Reports of the Secretary-General on the United Nations Observers Mission in Angola (MONUA)
Reports of the Secretary-General on the UN office in Angola (ONUA)

Meetings: **1997**: **3827, 3814**
1998: **3850, 3863, 3876, 3891, 3894, 3899, 3916, 3925, 3936, 3951**, 3960, **3962**
1999: 3965, 3969, **3983, 3999**, 4007, 4027, 4036, **4052**

2000: 4090, 4113, 4113 (Resumption 1), **4126,** 4129, **4129 (Resumption 1),** 4178, 4178 (Resumption 1)

Resolution 1127 (1997) of 28 August 1997
Resolution 1135 (1997) of 29 October 1997
Resolution 1149 (1998) of 27 January 1998
Resolution 1157 (1998) of 20 March 1998
Resolution 1164 (1998) of 29 April 1998
Resolution 1173 (1998) of 12 June 1998
Resolution 1176 (1998) of 24 June 1998
Resolution 1180 (1998) of 29 June 1998
Resolution 1190 (1998) of 13 August 1998
Resolution 1195 (1998) of 15 September 1998
Resolution 1202 (1998) of 15 October 1998
Resolution 1213 (1998) of 3 December 1998
Resolution 1219 (1998) of 31 December 1998
Resolution 1221 (1999) of 12 January 1999
Resolution 1229 (1999) of 26 February 1999
Resolution 1237 (1999) of 7 May 1999
Resolution 1268 (1999) of 15 October 1999
Resolution 1294 (2000) of 13 March 2000
Resolution 1295 (2000) of 18 April 2000

Statement, 23 December 1998
Statement, 21 January 1999
Statement, 19 May 1999
Statement, 24 August 1999

Letter dated 24 June 1998 from the Secretary-General addressed to the President of the Security Council

Letter dated 11 August 1999 from the Secretary-General addressed to the President of the Security Council

Letter dated 7 November 2000 from the Secretary-General addressed to the President of the Security Council

AF. 44 The Situation concerning Rwanda
Reports of the Secretary-General on the United Nations Observer Mission Uganda-Rwanda (UNOMIR)
Reports of the Secretary-General on the United Nations Assistance Mission for Rwanda (UNAMIR)
Reports of the Secretary-General on security in the Rwandese refugee camps
Reports of the Secretary-General on the Situation in Rwanda

Meetings: **1993**: **3183, 3244,** 3273, **3288, 3324**
1994: **3326,** 3337, **3358,** 3361, **3368,** 3371, **3377, 3388, 3391, 3392, 3400,** 3402, 3405, 3414, 3436, 3472, **3473,** 3481
1995: 3500, **3502, 3504,** 3526, **3542, 3555, 3566,** 3569, **3574,** 3588, **3604, 3605**
1996: **3640, 3656**
1998: **3870**
2000: 4127

Resolution 812 (1993) of 12 March 1993
Resolution 846 (1993) of 22 June 1993
Resolution 872 (1993) of 2 October 1993
Resolution 891 (1993) of 20 December 1993
Resolution 893 (1994) of 6 January 1994
Resolution 909 (1994) of 5 April 1994
Resolution 912 (1994) of 21 April 1994
Resolution 918 (1994) of 17 May 1994
Resolution 925 (1994) of 8 June 1994
Resolution 928 (1994) of 20 June 1994
Resolution 929 (1994) of 22 June 1994
Resolution 935 (1994) of 1 July 1994
Resolution 965 (1994) of 30 November 1994
Resolution 977 (1995) of 22 February 1995
Resolution 978 (1995) of 27 February 1995
Resolution 997 (1995) of 9 June 1995
Resolution 1005 (1995) of 17 July 1995
Resolution 1011 (1995) of 16 August 1995
Resolution 1013 (1995) of 7 September 1995
Resolution 1028 (1995) of 8 December 1995

Resolution 1029 (1995) of 12 December 1995
Resolution 1050 (1996) of 8 March 1996
Resolution 1053 (1996) of 23 April 1996
Resolution 1161 (1998) of 9 April 1998

Statement, 10 September 1993
Statement, 17 February 1994
Statement, 7 April 1994
Statement, 30 April 1994
Statement, 14 July 1994
Statement, 10 August 1994
Statement, 14 October 1994
Statement, 30 November 1994
Statement, 10 February 1995
Statement, 27 April 1995
Statement, 23 August 1995
Statement, 17 October 1995

Letter dated 6 May 1994 from the President of the Security Council addressed to the Secretary-General

Letter dated 13 February 1996 from the President of the Security Council addressed to the Secretary-General

Letter dated 13 February 1996 from the President of the Security Council addressed to the Secretary-General

Letter dated 13 March 1996 from the Secretary-General addressed to the President of the Security Council

Letter dated 14 March 1996 from the Secretary-General addressed to the President of the Security Council

Letter dated 27 September 1996 from the Secretary-General addressed to the President of the Security Council

Letter dated 1 November 1996 from the Secretary-General addressed to the President of the Security Council

Letter dated 22 January 1998 from the Secretary-General addressed to the President of the Security Council

Letter dated 27 May 1998 from the Secretary-General addressed to the President of the Security Council

Letter dated 18 March 1999 from the Secretary-General addressed to the President of the Security Council

Letter dated 26 March 1999 from the President of the Security Council addressed to the Secretary-General

Letter dated 15 December 1999 from the Secretary-General addressed to the President of the Security Council

AF. 45 Establishment of an International Tribunal for the prosecution of persons responsible for serious violations of International humanitarian law committed in the territory of Rwanda and Rwandan citizens responsible for such violations committed in the territory of neighbouring States

Meetings: **1994**: **3453**
1995: **3524**
1998: **3877**, 3908, 3917, **3934**
1999: **4006**, **4033**, 4063
2000: 4150, 4229, **4240**

Resolution 955 (1994) of 8 November 1994
Resolution 989 (1995) of 24 April 1995
Resolution 1165 (1998) of 30 April 1998
Resolution 1200 (1998) of 30 September 1998
Resolution 1241 (1999) of 19 May 1999
Resolution 1259 (1999) of 11 August 1999
Resolution 1329 (2000) of 30 November 2000

Identical letters dated 15 October 1997 from the Secretary-General addressed to the President of the General Assembly and the President of the Security Council

Letter dated 7 August 1998 from the Secretary-General addressed to the President of the Security Council

Letter dated 18 August 1998 from the President of the Security Council addressed to the Secretary-General

Letter dated 12 April 1999 from the Secretary-General addressed to the President of the Security Council

Letter dated 20 April 1999 from the President of the Security Council addressed to the Secretary-General

Letter dated 28 September 2000 from the Secretary-General addressed to the President of the Security Council

AF. 46 The Situation in the Great Lakes Region

Meetings: **1996**: 3708, **3710, 3713**
1997: 3738, **3741,** 3748, 3762, 3771, 3773

Resolution 1078 (1996) of 9 November 1996
Resolution 1080 (1996) of 15 November 1996
Resolution 1097 (1997) of 18 February 1997

Statement, 1 November 1996
Statement, 7 February 1997
Statement, 7 March 1997
Statement, 4 April 1997
Statement, 24 April 1997
Statement, 30 April 1997

Letter dated 29 October 1996 from the Secretary-General addressed to the President of the Security Council

Letter dated 30 December 1996 from the President of the Security Council addressed to the Secretary-General

Letter dated 22 January 1997 from the Secretary-General addressed to the President of the Security Council

Letter dated 18 February 1997 from the Secretary-General addressed to the President of the Security Council

Letter dated 12 December 1997 from the Secretary-General addressed to the President of the Security Council

Letter dated 29 December 1999 from the Secretary-General addressed to the President of the Security Council

Letter dated 26 September 2000 from the Secretary-General addressed to the President of the Security Council

AF. 47 The Situation in the Republic of Congo

Meetings: **1997**: 3810, 3823

Statement, 13 August 1997
Statement, 16 October 1997

Letter dated 20 June 1997 from the Secretary-General addressed to the President of the Security Council

AF. 48 The Situation in Zaire
The Situation concerning the Democratic Republic of Congo
Reports of the Secretary-General on the UN Preliminary Deployment in the Democratic Republic of the Congo
Reports of the Secretary-General on the UN Mission in the Democratic Republic of Congo (MONUC)
Security Council special mission visit to the Democratic Republic of Congo, 4-8 May 2000

Meetings: **1997**: 3784
1998: 3903, 3922, 3953
1999: 3987, 3987 (Resumption), **3993,** 4015, **4032, 4060, 4076,** 4083
2000: 4092, 4092 (Resumption 1), 4092 (Resumption 2), **4104,** 4132, 4135, 4143, 4143 (Resumption 1), 4151, 4156, 4157, 4158, **4159,** 4183, **4189,** 4194, **4207,** 4237, 4237, **4247**

Resolution 1234 (1999) of 9 April 1999
Resolution 1258 (1999) of 6 August 1999
Resolution 1273 (1999) of 5 November 1999
Resolution 1279 (1999) of 30 November 1999
Resolution 1291 (2000) of 24 February 2000
Resolution 1304 (2000) of 16 June 2000
Resolution 1316 (2000) of 23 August 2000
Resolution 1323 (2000) of 13 October 2000
Resolution 1332 (2000) of 14 December 2000

Statement, 29 May 1997
Statement, 13 July 1998
Statement, 31 August 1998
Statement, 11 December 1998
Statement, 24 June 1999
Statement, 24 January 2000
Statement, 5 May 2000
Statement, 2 June 2000
Statement, 7 September 2000

Letter dated 4 June 1996 from the Secretary-General addressed to the President of the Security Council

Letter dated 14 October 1996 from the Secretary-General addressed to the President of the Security Council

Letter dated 24 October 1996 from the Secretary-General addressed to the President of the Security Council

Letter dated 25 October 1996 from the President of the Security Council addressed to the Secretary-General

Letter dated 7 November 1996 from the Secretary-General addressed to the President of the Security Council

Letter dated 5 December 1996 from the Secretary-General addressed to the President of the Security Council

Letter dated 5 March 1997 from the Secretary-General addressed to the President of the Security Council

Letter dated 12 December 1997 from the Secretary-General addressed to the President of the Security Council

Letter dated 29 June 1998 from the Secretary-General addressed to the President of the Security Council

Letter dated 1 April 1999 from the Secretary-General addressed to the President of the Security Council

Letter dated 5 April 1999 from the President of the Security Council addressed to the Secretary-General

Letter dated 18 April 2000 from the Secretary-General addressed to the President of the Security Council

Letter dated 24 April 2000 from the President of the Security Council addressed to the Secretary-General

Letter dated 28 April 2000 ftom the President of the Security Council addressed to the Secretary-General

Letter dated 14 August 2000 from the Secretary-General addressed to the President of the Security Council

AF. 49 The Situation in Burundi

Meetings: **1993**: 3316
1994: 3410, 3419, 3441, 3485
1995: 3497, 3506, 3511, **3571**
1996: 3616, **3623, 3639,** 3659, 3664, 3684, 3692, **3695**
1997: 3785
1999: 4067, 4067 (Resumption 1), 4068
2000: **4091,** 4201, 4202

Resolution 1012 (1995) of 28 August 1995
Resolution 1041 (1996) of 29 January 1996
Resolution 1049 (1996) of 5 March 1996
Resolution 1072 (1996) of 30 August 1996
Resolution 1286 (2000) of 19 January 2000

Statement, 25 October 1993
Statement, 16 November 1993
Statement, 29 July 1994
Statement, 25 August 1994
Statement, 21 October 1994
Statement, 22 December 1994
Statement, 31 January 1995
Statement, 9 March 1995
Statement, 29 March 1995
Statement, 31 March 1995
Statement, 5 January 1996
Statement, 25 April 1996
Statement, 15 May 1996
Statement, 24 July 1996
Statement, 29 July 1996
Statement, 30 May 1997
Statement, 12 November 1999
Statement, 29 September 2000

Letter dated 3 January 1996 from the Secretary-General addressed to the President of the Security Council

Letter dated 12 January 1996 from the President of the Security Council addressed to the Secretary-General

Letter dated 16 January 1996 from the Secretary-General addressed to the President of the Security Council

Letter dated 12 April 1996 from the Secretary-General addressed to the President of the Security Council

Letter dated 22 July 1996 from the Secretary-General addressed to the President of the Security Council

Letter dated 24 September 1996 from the President of the Security Council addressed to the Secretary-General

Letter dated 23 June 1998 from the Secretary-General addressed to the President of the Security Council

Letter dated 30 June 1998 from the President of the Security Council addressed to the Secretary-General

Letter dated 15 October 1998 from the Secretary-General addressed to the President of the Security Council

Letter dated 11 November 1998 from the Secretary-General addressed to the President of the Security Council

Letter dated 17 November 1998 from the President of the Security Council addressed to the Secretary-General

Letter dated 2 November 1999 from the Secretary-General addressed to the President of the Security Council

AF. 50 The Situation in the Central African Republic
Reports of the Secretary-General on the United Nations Mission in the Central African Republic (MINURCA)

Meetings: **1997**: **3808, 3829**
1998: **3853, 3860, 3867, 3905, 3935**
1999: 3979, **3984, 4056**
2000: 4101

Resolution 1125 (1997) of 6 August 1997
Resolution 1136 (1997) of 6 November 1997
Resolution 1152 (1998) of 5 February 1998
Resolution 1155 (1998) of 16 March 1998
Resolution 1159 (1998) of 27 March 1998
Resolution 1182 (1998) of 14 July 1998
Resolution 1201 (1998) of 15 October 1998
Resolution 1230 (1999) of 26 February 1999
Resolution 1271 (1999) of 22 October 1999

Statement, 18 February 1999
Statement, 10 February 2000

Letter dated 3 December 1999 from the Secretary-General addressed to the President of the Security Council

Letter dated 10 December 1999 from the President of the Security Council addressed to the Secretary-General

Letter dated 28 September 2000 from the Secretary-General addressed to the President of the Security Council.

Letter dated 3 October 2000 from the President of the Security Council addressed to the Secretary-General.

AF. 51 The Situation in Sierra Leone
Reports of the Secretary-General on the United Nations Observers Mission in Sierra Leone (UNOMSIL)
Reports of the Secretary-General pursuant to Security Council Resolution 1270 (1999) on the United Nations Mission in Sierra Leone (UNAMSIL)

Meetings: **1995**: 3597
1996: 3632, 3643, 3720
1997: 3781, 3797, 3798, 3809, **3822,** 3834
1998: 3857, **3861, 3872,** 3882, **3889, 3902,** 3957
1999: 3963, **3964, 3986,** 4005, **4012, 4035, 4054,** 4078
2000: 4098, **4099,** 4111, 4111 (Resumption 1), 4134, 4139, **4145,** 4163, **4168,** 4173, **4184, 4186, 4193, 4199,** 4216, **4253**

Resolution 1132 (1997) of 8 October 1997
Resolution 1156 (1998) of 16 March 1998
Resolution 1162 (1998) of 17 April 1998
Resolution 1171 (1998) of 5 June 1998
Resolution 1181 (1998) of 13 July 1998
Resolution 1220 (1999) of 12 January 1999
Resolution 1231 (1999) of 11 March 1999
Resolution 1245 (1999) of 11 June 1999
Resolution 1260 (1999) of 20 August 1999
Resolution 1270 (1999) of 22 October 1999
Resolution 1289 (2000) of 7 February 2000
Resolution 1299 (2000) of 19 May 2000
Resolution 1306 (2000) of 5 June 2000
Resolution 1313 (2000) of 4 August 2000
Resolution 1315 (2000) of 14 August 2000
Resolution 1317 (2000) of 5 September 2000
Resolution 1321 (2000) of 20 September 2000
Resolution 1334 (2000) of 22 December 2000

Statement, 27 November 1995
Statement, 15 February 1996
Statement, 19 March 1996
Statement, 4 December 1996

Statement, 27 May 1997
Statement, 11 July 1997
Statement, 11 July 1997
Statement, 6 August 1997
Statement, 14 November 1997
Statement, 2 February 1998
Statement, 26 February 1998
Statement, 20 May 1998
Statement, 7 January 1999
Statement, 15 May 1999
Statement, 4 May 2000
Statement, 17 July 2000
Statement, 3 November 2000

Communique of 21 June 2000

Letter dated 13 December 1996 from the Secretary-General addressed to the President of the Security Council

Letter dated 17 December 1996 from the President of the Security Council addressed to the Secretary-General

Letter dated 7 October 1997 from the Secretary-General addressed to the President of the Security Council

Letter dated 20 February 1998 from the Secretary-General addressed to the President of the Security Council

Letter dated 3 August 1998 from the Secretary-General addressed to the President of the Security Council

Letter dated 5 August 1998 from the President of the Security Council addressed to the Secretary-General

Letter dated 17August 1998 from the Secretary-General addressed to the President of the Security Council

Letter dated 23 December 1999 from the Secretary-General addressed to the President of the Security Council

Letter dated 17 May 2000 from the Secretary-General addressed to the President of the Security Council

AF. 52 The Situation in Africa
Causes of conflict and the promotion of durable peace and sustainable development in Africa
The impact of AIDS on peace and security in Africa

Meetings: **1997**: 3819
1998: 3871, 3875, 3875 (Resumption 1), **3886, 3927, 3928,** 3931, **3945,** 3950
1999: 4047, 4049, 4049 (Resumption 1), 4049 (Resumption 2), 4049 (Resumption 3), 4081, 4081 (Resumption 1)
2000: 4087, 4096

Resolution 1170 (1998) of 28 May 1998
Resolution 1196 (1998) of 16 September 1998
Resolution 1197 (1998) of 18 September 1998
Resolution 1208 (1998) of 19 November 1998
Resolution 1209 (1998) of 19 November 1998

Statement, 25 September 1997
Statement, 16 September 1998
Statement, 24 September 1998
Statement, 30 November 1998

Letter dated 2 November 1999 from the Secretary-General addressed to the President of the Security Council

Letter dated 5 November 1999 from the President of the Security Council addressed to the Secretary-General

Letter dated 31 January 2000 from the President of the Security Council to the Secretary-General

AF. 53 The situation between Ertitrea and Ethiopia
Security Council Special Mission visit to Eritrea and Ethiopia, 9-10 May 2000

Meetings: **1998**: **3895**
1999: **3973**, **3975**, 3985
2000: **4142**, **4144**, **4181**, 4187, **4197**

Resolution 1177 (1998) of 26 June 1998
Resolution 1226 (1999) of 29 January 1999
Resolution 1227 (1999) of 10 February 1999
Resolution 1297 (2000) of 12 May 2000
Resolution 1298 (2000) of 17 May 2000
Resolution 1312 (2000) of 31 July 2000
Resolution 1320 (2000) of 15 September 2000

Statement, 27 February 1999

Letter dated 7 May 2000 from the President of the Security Council addressed to the Secretary-General

Letter dated 7 July 2000 from the President of the Security Council addressed to the Secretary-General

Letter dated 21 September 2000 from the Secretary-General addressed to the President of the Security-Council

AF. 54 The situation in Guinea-Bissau
Reports of the Secretary-General on the United Nations Peacebuilding Support Office in Guinea-Bissau (UNOGBIS)

Meetings: **1998**: 3940, **3958**
1999: **3991**
2000: 4121, 4121 (Resumption 1), 4122, 4238, 4238 (Resumption 1), 4239

Resolution 1216 (1998) of 21 December 1998
Resolution 1233 (1999) of 6 April 1999

Statement, 6 November 1998
Statement, 29 March 2000
Statement, 29 November 2000

Letter dated 26 February 1999 from the Secretary-General addressed to the President of the Security Council

Letter dated 3 March 1999 from the President of the Security Council addressed to the Secretary-General

Letter dated 28 June 1999 from the Secretary-General addressed to the President of the Security Council

Letter dated 30 June 1999 from the President of the Security Council addressed to the Secretary-General

Letter dated 13 October 1999 from the Secretary-General addressed to the President of the Security Council

Letter dated 26 October 1999 from the President of the Security Council addressed to the Secretary-General

Letter dated 9 December 1999 from the Secretary-General addressed to the President of the Security Council

Letter dated 14 December 1999 from the President of the Security Council addressed to the Secretary-General

Letter dated 3 March 2000 from the Secretary-General addressed to the President of the Security Council

Letter dated 10 March 2000 from the President of the Security Council addressed to the Secretary-General

Letter dated 28 September 2000 from the Secretary-General addressed to the President of the Security Council

Letter dated 3 October 2000 from the President of the Security Council addressed to the Secretary-General

AF. 55 Promoting peace and security-humanitarian assistance to refugees in Africa

Meeting: **2000:** 4089

Statement, 13 January 2000

AF. 56 Ensuring an effective role of the Security Council in the maintenance of international peace and security, particularly in Africa

Meeting: **2000: 4194**

Resolution 1318 (2000) of 7 September 2000

Presidential Note, 2 August 2000

AF. 57 The situation in Guinea following recent attacks along its borders with Liberia and Sierra Leone

Meeting: **2000**: 4252

Statement, 21 December 2000

5

ASIA

AS. 01 The Iranian question

Meetings: **1946**: 2, 3, **5,** 26, 27, 28, 29, **30,** 32, 33, 36, **40**, 43.

Resolution 2 (1946) of 30 January 1946
Resolution 3 (1946) of 4 April 1946
Resolution 5 (1946) of 8 May 1946

Decision, 29 March 1946

AS. 02 The Indonesian question

Meetings: **1946**: 2
1947: 171, 172, **173,** 174, 178, 181, 184, 185, 187, 192, 193, **194, 195,** 206, **207,** 208, 209, 210, 211, 212, 213, 214, 215, 216, 217, 218, **219,** 222, 224, 225.
1948: 229, 247, 248, 249, 251, 252, 256, **259,** 316, 322, 323, 326, 328, 329, 341, **342,** 387, 388, 389, 390, 391, **392,** 393, **395,** 396.
1949: 397, 398, 400, 401, 402, 403, 404, 405, **406,** 410, 416, 417, 418, 419, 420, 421, 454, 455, 456.

Resolution 27 (1947) of 1August 1947
Resolution 30 (1947) of 25 August 1947
Resolution 31 (1947) of 25 August 1947
Resolution 32 (1947) of 26 August 1947
Resolution 35 (1947) of 3 October 1947
Resolution 36 (1947) of 1 November 1947

K. Wellens (ed.),
Resolutions and Statements of the United Nations Security Council (1946-2000), 75–106.

Resolution 40 (1948) of 28 February 1948
Resolution 41 (1948) of 28 February 1948
Resolution 55 (1948) of 29 July 1948
Resolution 63 (1948) of 24 December 1948
Resolution 64 (1948) of 28 December 1948
Resolution 65 (1948) of 28 December 1948
Resolution 67 (1949) of 28 January 1949

Message, 23 March 1949

AS. 03 Complaint of aggression upon the Republic of Korea

Meetings: **1950**: **473, 474,** 475, **476,** 477, 478, **479,** 480, 481, 482, 483, 484, 485, 486, 487, 488, 489, 490, 492, 493, 494, 495, 496, 497, 502, 503, 508, 518, 519, **520,** 521, 523, 524, 525, 526, 527, 528, 529, 530.
1951: **531.**

Resolution 82 (1950) of 25 June 1950
Resolution 83 (1950) of 27 June 1950
Resolution 84 (1950) of 7 July 1950
Resolution 85 (1950) of 31 July 1950
Resolution 88 (1950) of 8 November 1950
Resolution 90 (1951) of 31 January 1951

AS. 04 Complaint of armed invasion of Taiwan (Formosa)

Meetings: **1950**: 490, 492, 493, 494, 495, 496, 497, 498, 499, 501, 502, 503, 504, 505, **506,** 507, 525, 526, 527, 528, 529, 530.

Resolution 87 (1950) of 29 September 1950

AS. 05 Question relating to Laos

Meetings: **1959**: 847, **848**

Resolution 132 (1959) of 7 September 1959

AS. 06 Reports of the Secretary-General to the Security Council concerning developments relating to Yemen

Meetings: **1963**: 1037, 1038, **1039.**

Resolution 179 (1963) of 11 June 1963

AS. 07 Complaint by Yemen against the United Kingdom

Meetings: **1964**: 1106, 1107, 1108, 1109, 1110, **1111**.

Resolution 188 (1964) of 9 April 1964

AS. 08 The Cyprus Question
The Situation in Cyprus
Reports of the Secretary-General on the United Nations Force in Cyprus (UNFICYP)
Reports of the Secretary-General on his mission of good offices in Cyprus
Reports of the Secretary-General on the UN operations in Cyprus

Meetings: **1963**: 1085
1964: 1094, 1095, 1096, 1097, 1098, 1099, 1100, 1101, **1102, 1103,** 1136, 1137, 1138, **1139,** 1142, 1143, 1151, 1153, 1154, 1155, 1156, 1157, 1158, **1159, 1180**
1965: 1191, 1192, **1193, 1224,** 1234, 1235, **1236,** 1252, **1270**
1966: 1274, **1275, 1286, 1338**
1967: **1362,** 1383, 1385, **1386**
1968: **1398, 1432, 1459**
1969: **1474, 1521**
1970: **1543, 1564**
1971: **1567**, 1568, **1612,** 1613
1972: **1646,** 1647, **1683**
1973: **1727**, 1728, **1759**

1974: 1771, **1772, 1779, 1780,** 1781, **1782,** 1783, 1784, 1785, 1786, 1787, 1788, **1789, 1792, 1793, 1794, 1795, 1810**
1975: 1813, 1814, 1815, 1816, 1817, 1818, 1819, **1820, 1830,** 1831, **1863**
1976: **1925, 1926,** 1927, 1979, **1980**
1977: **2012,** 2013, 2026, 2027, 2028, 2029, 2030, 2031, **2032, 2054,** 2055
1978: **2080,** 2081, 2099, **2100, 2107**
1979: **2150, 2179**
1980: **2230, 2257**
1981: **2279, 2313**
1982: **2378, 2405**
1983: **2453,** 2454, 2497, 2498, 2499, **2500, 2503**
1984: 2531, 2532, 2533, 2534, 2535, 2536, 2537, 2538, **2539, 2547, 2565**
1985: **2591, 2635**
1986: **2688,** 2689, **2729**
1987: **2749, 2771**
1988: **2816, 2833**
1989: **2868, 2898**
1990: **2909, 2928,** 2930, **2969, 2971**
1991: **2992, 2993, 3013, 3022,** 3024.
1992: **3067, 3084,** 3094, **3109, 3140, 3148**
1993: 3211, **3222, 3235**
1994: **3347, 3390, 3412, 3484**
1995: **3547, 3608**
1996: **3675, 3728**
1997: **3794, 3846**
1998: **3898, 3959**
1999: **4018, 4082**
2000: **4155, 4246**

Resolution 186 (1964) of 4 March 1964
Resolution 187 (1964) of 13 March 1964
Resolution 192 (1964) of 20 June 1964
Resolution 193 (1964) of 9 August 1964
Resolution 194 (1964) of 25 September 1964
Resolution 198 (1964) of 18 December 1964

Resolution 201 (1965) of 19 March 1965
Resolution 206 (1965) of 15 June 1965
Resolution 207 (1965) of 10 August 1965
Resolution 219 (1965) of 17 December 1965
Resolution 220 (1966) of 16 March 1966
Resolution 222 (1966) of 16 June 1966
Resolution 231 (1966) of 15 December 1966
Resolution 238 (1967) of 19 June 1967
Resolution 244 (1967) of 22 December 1967
Resolution 247 (1968) of 18 March 1968
Resolution 254 (1968) of 18 June 1968
Resolution 261 (1968) of 10 December 1968
Resolution 266 (1969) of 10 June 1969
Resolution 274 (1969) of 11 December 1969
Resolution 281 (1970) of 9 June 1970
Resolution 291 (1970) of 10 December 1970
Resolution 293 (1971) of 26 May 1971
Resolution 305 (1971) of 13 December 1971
Resolution 315 (1972) of 15 June 1972
Resolution 324 (1972) of 12 December 1972
Resolution 334 (1973) of 15 June 1973
Resolution 343 (1973) of 14 December 1973
Resolution 349 (1974) of 29 May 1974
Resolution 353 (1974) of 20 July 1974
Resolution 354 (1974) of 23 July 1974
Resolution 355 (1974) of 1 August 1974
Resolution 357 (1974) of 14 August 1974
Resolution 358 (1974) of 15 August 1974
Resolution 359 (1974) of 15 August 1974
Resolution 360 (1974) of 16 August 1974
Resolution 361 (1974) of 30 August 1974
Resolution 364 (1974) of 13 December 1974
Resolution 365 (1974) of 13 December 1974
Resolution 367 (1975) of 12 March 1975
Resolution 370 (1975) of 13 June 1975
Resolution 383 (1975) of 13 December 1975
Resolution 391 (1976) of 15 June 1976
Resolution 401 (1976) of 14 December 1976

Resolution 410 (1977) of 15 June 1977
Resolution 414 (1977) of 15 September 1977
Resolution 422 (1977) of 15 December 1977
Resolution 430 (1978) of 16 June 1978
Resolution 440 (1978) of 27 November 1978
Resolution 443 (1978) of 14 December 1978
Resolution 451 (1979) of 15 June 1979
Resolution 458 (1979) of 14 December 1979
Resolution 472 (1980) of 13 June 1980
Resolution 482 (1980) of 11 December 1980
Resolution 486 (1981) of 4 June 1981
Resolution 495 (1981) of 14 December 1981
Resolution 510 (1982) of 15 June 1982
Resolution 526 (1982) of 14 December 1982
Resolution 534 (1983) of 15 June 1983
Resolution 541 (1983) of 18 November 1983
Resolution 544 (1983) of 15 December 1983
Resolution 550 (1984) of 11 May 1984
Resolution 553 (1984) of 15 June 1984
Resolution 559 (1984) of 14 December 1984
Resolution 565 (1985) of 14 June 1985
Resolution 578 (1985) of 12 December 1985
Resolution 585 (1986) of 13 June 1986
Resolution 593 (1986) of 11 December 1986
Resolution 597 (1987) of 12 June 1987
Resolution 604 (1987) of 14 December 1987
Resolution 614 (1988) of 15 June 1988
Resolution 625 (1988) of 15 December 1988
Resolution 634 (1989) of 9 June 1989
Resolution 646 (1989) of 14 December 1989
Resolution 649 (1990) of 12 March 1990
Resolution 657 (1990) of 15 June 1990
Resolution 680 (1990) of 14 December 1990
Resolution 682 (1990) of 21 December 1990
Resolution 697 (1991) of 14 June 1991
Resolution 698 (1991) of 14 June 1991
Resolution 716 (1991) of 11 October 1991
Resolution 723 (1991) of 12 December 1991

Resolution 750 (1992) of 10 April 1992
Resolution 759 (1992) of 12 June 1992
Resolution 774 (1992) of 26 August 1992
Resolution 789 (1992) of 25 November 1992
Resolution 796 (1992) of 14 December 1992
Resolution 831 (1993) of 27 May 1993
Resolution 839 (1993) of 11 June 1993
Resolution 889 (1993) of 15 December 1993
Resolution 902 (1994) of 11 March 1994
Resolution 927 (1994) of 15 June 1994
Resolution 939 (1994) of 29 July 1994
Resolution 969 (1994) of 21 December 1994
Resolution 1000 (1995) of 23 June 1995
Resolution 1032 (1995) of 19 December 1995
Resolution 1062 (1996) of 28 June 1996
Resolution 1092 (1996) of 23 December 1996
Resolution 1117 (1997) of 27 June 1997
Resolution 1146 (1997) of 23 December 1997
Resolution 1178 (1998) of 29 June 1998
Resolution 1179 (1998) of 29 June 1998
Resolution 1217 (1998) of 22 December 1998
Resolution 1218 (1998) of 22 December 1998
Resolution 1250 (1999) of 29 June 1999
Resolution 1251 (1999) of 29 June 1999
Resolution 1283 (1999) of 15 December 1999
Resolution 1303 (2000) of 14 June 2000
Resolution 1331 (2000) of 13 December 2000

Statement, 11 August 1964
Statement, 20 September 1985
Statement, 15 December 1988
Statement, 9 June 1989
Statement, 14 December 1989
Statement, 22 February 1990
Statement, 15 June 1990
Statement, 19 July 1990
Statement, 9 November 1990
Statement, 28 March 1991

Statement, 28 June 1991
Statement, 12 December 1991
Statement, 23 December 1991
Statement, 13 July 1992
Statement, 26 March 1993

Letter dated 28 September 1992 from the President of the Security Council addressed to the Secretary-General

Letter dated 7 July 1993 from the President of the Security Council addressed to the Secretary-General

Letter dated 20 September 1993 from the President of the Security Council addressed to the Secretary-General

Letter dated 11 April 1994 from the President of the Security Council addressed to the Secretary-General

Letter dated 20 June 1997 from the Secretary-General addressed to the President of the Security Council

Letter dated 20 April 1998 from the Secretary-General addressed to the President of the Security Council

Letter dated 14 December 1998 from the Secretary-General addressed to the President of the Security Council

AS. 09 Complaint concerning acts of aggression against the territory and civilian population of Cambodia

Meetings: **1964**: 1118, 1119, 1120, 1121, 1122, 1124, 1125, **1126.**

Resolution 189 (1964) of 4 June 1964

AS. 10 The question of Bahrain

Meetings: **1970**: 1536.

Resolution 278 (1970) of 11 May 1970

AS. 11 The India-Pakistan question

Meetings: **1948**: 226, 227, 228, **229, 230,** 231, 232, 234, 235, 236, 237, 239, 240, 241, 242, 243, 244, 245, 246, 250, 257, 264, 266, 269, 284, 285, **286,** 287, 289, 290, 304, 305, 311, **312,** 315, 356, 382.
1950: 463, 464, 465, 466, 467, 468, 469, **470,** 471.
1951: 532, 533, 534, 535, 536, 537, 538, **539,** 540, 543, 548, 564, **566.**
1952: 570, 571, 572, 605, 606, 607, 608, 609, 610, 611.
1957: 761, 762, 763, 764, **765,** 766, 767, 768, 769, 770, 771, 772, 773, **774,** 791, 795, 796, 797, 798, 799, 800, 801, 802. 803, 804, 805, 807, **808.**
1965: **1237, 1238,** 1239, 1240, 1241, **1242,** 1244, **1245,** 1247, 1248, 1249, **1251.**

Resolution 38 (1948) of 17 January 1948
Resolution 39 (1948) of 20 January 1948
Resolution 47 (1948) of 21 April 1948
Resolution 51 (1948) of 3 June 1948
Resolution 80 (1948) of 14 March 1950
Resolution 91 (1948) of 30 March 1951
Resolution 96 (1951) of 10 November 1951
Resolution 98 (1952) of 23 December 1952
Resolution 122 (1957) of 24 January 1957
Resolution 123 (1957) of 21 February 1957
Resolution 126 (1957) of 2 December 1957
Resolution 209 (1965) of 4 September 1965
Resolution 210 (1965) of 6 September 1965
Resolution 211 (1965) of 20 September 1965

Resolution 214 (1965) of 27 September 1965
Resolution 215 (1965) of 5 November 1965

Decision, 25 November 1948

Letter approved on 29 May 1951 by the Security Council and to be sent by the President to the Governments of India and Pakistan

Statement, 22 September 1965

AS. 12 The situation in the India Pakistan subcontinent

Meetings: **1971**: 1606, 1607, **1608,** 1611, 1614, 1615, 1616, 1617, **1621.**

Resolution 303 (1971) of 6 December 1971
Resolution 307 (1971) of 21 December 1971

AS. 13 The situation in Timor

Meetings: **1975**: 1864, 1865, 1867, **1868,** 1869.
1976: 1908, 1909, 1910, 1911, 1912, 1913, 1914, **1915.**

Resolution 384 (1975) of 22 December 1975
Resolution 389 (1976) of 22 April 1976

Letter dated 21 June 1976 from the President of the Security Council and addressed to the Permanent Representative of Indonesia to the United Nations.

AS. 14 Complaint by Iraq concerning incidents on its frontier with Iran

Meetings: **1974**: 1762, 1763, 1764, **1770.**

Resolution 348 (1974) of 28 May 1974

Statement, 28 February 1974

AS. 15 Complaint by Iraq against Israel

Meetings: **1981**: 2280, 2281, 2282, 2283, 2284, 2285, 2286, 2287, **2288**.

Resolution 487 (1981) of 19 June 1981

AS. 16 The situation between Iran and Iraq

Meetings: **1980**: 2247, **2248**, 2250, 2251, 2252, 2253, 2254.
1982: **2383, 2399.**
1983: **2493.**
1986: 2663, 2664, 2665, **2666**, 2667, 2709, 2710, 2711, 2712, **2713**, 2730.
1987: 2732, 2733, 2734, 2735, 2736, 2737, 2738, **2750**, 2779, 2798.
1988: **2812**, 2823, **2824, 2825.**
1989: 2844, 2885.
1990: 2908, 2916, 2944, 2961
1991: 2976

Resolution 479 (1980) of 28 September 1980
Resolution 514 (1982) of 12 July 1982
Resolution 522 (1982) of 4 October 1982
Resolution 540 (1983) of 31 October 1983
Resolution 582 (1986) of 24 February 1986
Resolution 588 (1986) of 8 October 1986
Resolution 598 (1987) of 20 July 1987
Resolution 612 (1988) of 9 May 1988
Resolution 619 (1988) of 9 August 1988
Resolution 620 (1988) of 26 August 1988
Resolution 631 (1989) of 8 February 1989
Resolution 642 (1989) of 29 September 1989
Resolution 651 (1990) of 29 March 1990
Resolution 671 (1990) of 27 September 1990
Resolution 676 (1990) of 28 November 1990
Resolution 685 (1991) of 31 January 1991

Statement, 23 September 1980
Statement, 5 November 1980
Statement, 15 July 1982
Statement, 21 February 1983
Statement, 30 March 1984
Statement, 5 March 1985
Statement, 15 March 1985
Statement, 25 April 1985
Statement, 21 March 1986
Statement, 22 December 1986
Statement, 16 January 1987
Statement, 14 May 1987
Statement, 24 December 1987
Statement, 16 March 1988
Statement Secretary-General, 8 August 1988
Statement, 8 August 1988
Statement, 27 February 1990

Letter dated 14 June 1984 from the Secretary-General and addressed to the President of the Security Council

Letter dated 15 June 1984 from the President of the Security Council and addressed to the Secretary-General

Letter dated 27 October 1993 from the President of the Security Council addressed to the Secretary-General

AS. 17 Complaint by several Arab States against Iran

Meetings: **1984**: 2541, 2542, 2543, 2545, **2546.**

Resolution 552 (1984) of 1 June 1984

Letter dated 21 May 1984 from the representatives of Bahrain, Kuwait, Oman, Quatar, Saudi Arabia and the United Arab Emirates addressed to the President of the Security Council

AS. 18 Complaint by the United States of America against Iran (Hostages)

Meetings: **1979**: 2172, 2175, 2176, 2177, **2178,** 2182, 2183, **2184,** 2191.

Resolution 457 (1979) of 4 December 1979
Resolution 461 (1979) of 31 December 1979

Statement, 9 November 1979

Letter dated 25 november 1979 from the secretary-general to the President of the Security Council

Letter dated 22 december 1979 from the permanent representative of the United States of America to the United Nations addressed to the President of the Security Council

AS. 19 The Situation relating to Afghanistan
The Situation in Afghanistan

Meetings: **1980**: 2185, 2186, 2187, 2188, 2189, **2190.**
1988: **2828.**
1989: 2852, 2853, 2855, 2856, 2857, 2859, 2860.
1990: **2904.**
1994: 3330, 3353, 3415, 3474.
1996: 3631, 3648, 3650, 3699, 3705, **3706.**
1997: 3765, 3765 (Resumption 1), 3765 (Resumption 2), 3766, 3796, 3841.
1998: 3869, 3906, 3914, 3921, **3921 (Resumption),** 3926, **3952.**
1999: 4039, 4039 (Resumption 1), **4051,** 4055.
2000: 4124, 4125, **4251.**

Resolution 462 (1980) of 9 January 1980
Resolution 622 (1988) of 31 October 1988
Resolution 647 (1990) of 11 January 1990
Resolution 1076 (1996) of 22 October 1996
Resolution 1193 (1998) of 28 August 1998
Resolution 1214 (1998) of 8 December 1998

Resolution 1267 (1999) of 15 October 1999
Resolution 1333 (2000) of 19 December 2000

Statement, 16 April 1992
Statement, 12 August 1992
Statement, 24 January 1994
Statement, 23 March 1994
Statement, 11 August 1994
Statement, 30 November 1994
Statement, 15 February 1996
Statement, 28 September 1996
Statement, 16 April 1997
Statement, 9 July 1997
Statement, 16 December 1997
Statement, 6 April 1998
Statement, 14 July 1998
Statement, 6 August 1998
Statement, 15 September 1998
Statement, 22 October 1999
Statement, 7 April 2000

Letter dated 22 August 1996 from the President of the Security Council addressed to the Secretary-General

Letter dated 20 November 1996 from the Secretary-General addressed to the President of the Security Council

Letter dated 17 December 1996 from the President of the Security Council addressed to the Secretary-General

Letter dated 1 May 1997 from the Secretary-General addressed to the President of the Security Council

Letter dated 13 May 1997 from the President of the Security Council addressed to the Secretary-General

Letter dated 28 July 1997 from the Secretary-General addressed to the President of the Security Council

Letter dated 23 November 1998 from the Secretary-General addressed to the President of the Security Council

Letter dated 14 January 2000 from the Secretary-General addressed to the President of the Security Council

AS. 20 Complaint by Seychelles

Meetings: **1981**: **2314.**
1982: 2359, 2361, 2365, 2367, **2370.**

Resolution 496 (1981) of 15 December 1981
Resolution 507 (1982) of 28 May 1982

AS. 21 Complaint by Iran against the United States of America (Airbus)

Meetings: **1988**: 2818, 2819, 2820, **2821.**

Resolution 616 (1988) of 20 July 1988

Letter dated 5 July 1988 from the acting permanent representative of the Islamic Republic of Iran to the United Nations addressed to the President of the Security Council

AS. 22 The Situation in Cambodja

Meetings: **1990**: **2941.**
1991: **3014, 3015.**
1992: **3029, 3057**, 3085, **3099, 3124, 3143**, 3153
1993: **3181**, 3193, **3213**, 3214, **3227**, 3230, **3270**, 3287, **3303**
1997: 3799

Resolution 668 (1990) of 20 September 1990
Resolution 717 (1991) of 16 October 1991
Resolution 718 (1991) of 31 October 1991

Resolution 728 (1992) of 8 January 1992
Resolution 745 (1992) of 28 February 1992
Resolution 766 (1992) of 21 July 1992
Resolution 783 (1992) of 13 October 1992
Resolution 792 (1992) of 30 November 1992
Resolution 810 (1993) of 8 March 1993
Resolution 826 (1993) of 20 May 1993
Resolution 835 (1993) of 2 June 1993
Resolution 840 (1993) of 15 June 1993
Resolution 860 (1993) of 27 August 1993
Resolution 880 (1993) of 4 November 1993

Statement, 2 December 1992
Statement, 22 December 1992
Statement, 5 April 1993
Statement, 22 May 1993
Statement, 8 June 1993
Statement, 5 October 1993
Statement, 11 July 1997

Exchange of letters dated 2 and 3 August 1989 between the Secretary-General and the President of the Security Council concerning the dispatch of a fact-finding mission to Cambodia

Letter dated 26 July 1993 from the President of the Security Council addressed to the Secretary-General

Identical letters dated 23 June 1997 from the Secretary-General addressed to the President of the General Assembly and to the President of the Security Council

Letter dated 27 October 1997 from the Secretary-General addressed to the President of the Security Council

Letter dated 30 October 1997 from the President of the Security Council addressed to the Secretary-General

Letter dated 19 October 1998 from the Secretary-General addressed to the President of the Security Council

Letter dated 22 October 1998 from the President of the Security Council addressed to the Secretary-General

Identical letters dated 15 March 1999 from the Secretary-General addressed to the President of the General Assembly and to the President of the Security Council

AS. 23 The Situation between Iraq and Kuwait
Reports of the Secretary-General pursuant to paragraphs 28 en 30 of Security Council Resolution 1284 (1999) and pursuant to paragraphs 5 of Security Council Resolution 1281 (1999)
Reports of the Secretary-General pursuant to paragraph 5 of Security Council Resolution 1302 (2000)

Meetings: **1961**: 957, 958, 959, 960
1990: 2932, 2933, 2934, 2937, 2938, 2939, 2940, 2942, 2943, **2950**, 2951, **2959, 2960,** 2962, 2963
1991: 2977, Parts I and II, **2978,** 2979, **2981, 2983,** 2985, **2987, 2994,** 2995, 2996, **3004, 3008, 3012**
1992: 3058, 3059, 3059 (Resumption I and II), 3061, 3098, 3105, **3108,** 3112, **3117,** 3139, 3139 (Resumption 1), 3139 (Resumption 2)
1993: 3161, 3162, **3171, 3224,** 3242, 3245, 3246, 3319
1994: **3343,** 3435, **3438,** 3439, 3459
1995: **3519**
1996: 3642, **3644, 3672,** 3674, 3691, 3729
1997: 3768, **3786,** 3789, **3792, 3817, 3826,** 3828, **3831,** 3832, 3838, **3840,** 3844
1998: 3848, **3855, 3858, 3865,** 3880, **3893, 3924, 3939, 3946,** 3955
1999: **4008, 4050, 4070, 4077, 4079, 4084**
2000: 4120, **4123, 4152, 4241**

Resolution 660 (1990) of 2 August 1990
Resolution 661 (1990) of 6 August 1990

Resolution 662 (1990) of 9 August 1990
Resolution 664 (1990) of 18 August 1990
Resolution 665 (1990) of 25 August 1990
Resolution 666 (1990) of 13 September 1990
Resolution 667 (1990) of 16 September 1990
Resolution 669 (1990) of 24 September 1990
Resolution 670 (1990) of 25 September 1990
Resolution 674 (1990) of 29 October 1990
Resolution 677 (1990) of 28 November 1990
Resolution 678 (1990) of 29 November 1990
Resolution 686 (1991) of 2 March 1991
Resolution 687 (1991) of 3 April 1991
Resolution 689 (1991) of 9 April 1991
Resolution 692 (1991) of 20 May 1991
Resolution 699 (1991) of 17 June 1991
Resolution 700 (1991) of 17 June 1991
Resolution 705 (1991) of 15 August 1991
Resolution 706 (1991) of 15 August 1991
Resolution 707 (1991) of 15 August 1991
Resolution 712 (1991) of 19 September 1991
Resolution 715 (1991) of 11 October 1991
Resolution 773 (1992) of 26 August 1992
Resolution 778 (1992) of 2 October 1992
Resolution 806 (1993) of 5 February 1993
Resolution 833 (1993) of 27 May 1993
Resolution 899 (1994) of 4 March 1994
Resolution 949 (1994) of 15 October 1994
Resolution 986 (1995) of 14 April 1995
Resolution 1051 (1996) of 27 March 1996
Resolution 1060 (1996) of 12 June 1996
Resolution 1111 (1997) of 21 June 1997
Resolution 1115 (1997) of 21 June 1997
Resolution 1129 (1997) of 12 September 1997
Resolution 1134 (1997) of 23 October 1997
Resolution 1137 (1997) of 12 November 1997
Resolution 1143 (1997) of 4 December 1997
Resolution 1153 (1998) of 20 February 1998
Resolution 1154 (1998) of 2 March 1998

Resolution 1158 (1998) of 25 March 1998
Resolution 1175 (1998) of 19 June 1998
Resolution 1194 (1998) of 9 September 1998
Resolution 1205 (1998) of 5 November 1998
Resolution 1210 (1998) of 24 November 1998
Resolution 1242 (1999) of 21 May 1999
Resolution 1266 (1999) of 4 October 1999
Resolution 1275 (1999) of 19 November 1999
Resolution 1280 (1999) of 3 December 1999
Resolution 1281 (1999) of 10 December 1999
Resolution 1284 (1999) of 17 December 1999
Resolution 1293 (2000) of 31 March 2000
Resolution 1302 (2000) of 8 June 2000
Resolution 1330 (2000) of 5 December 2000

Statement, 3 March 1991
Statement, 2 October 1991
Statement, 29 April 1991
Statement, 28 June 1991
Statement, 20 December 1991
Statement, 5 February 1992
Statement, 19 February 1992
Statement, 28 February 1992
Statement, 11 March 1992
Statement, 12 March 1992
Statement, 19 March 1992
Statement, 27 March 1992
Statement, 10 April 1992
Statement, 27 May 1992
Statement, 17 June 1992
Statement, 6 July 1992
Statement, 17 July 1992
Statement, 27 July 1992
Statement, 2 September 1992
Statement, 24 September 1992
Statement, 23 November 1992
Statement, 24 November 1992
Statement, 24 November 1992

Statement, 8 January 1993
Statement, 11 January 1993
Statement, 25 January 1993
Statement, 29 March 1993
Statement, 24 May 1993
Statement, 18 June 1993
Statement, 28 June 1993
Statement, 21 July 1993
Statement, 20 September 1993
Statement, 18 November 1993
Statement, 23 November 1993
Statement, 8 October 1994
Statement, 16 November 1994
Statement, 19 March 1996
Statement, 14 June 1996
Statement, 23 August 1996
Statement, 30 December 1996
Statement, 16 April 1997
Statement, 13 June 1997
Statement, 29 October 1997
Statement, 13 November 1997
Statement, 3 December 1997
Statement, 22 December 1997
Statement, 14 January 1998
Statement, 14 May 1998

Presidential Note, 30 January 1999

Letter dated 6 August 1991 from the President of the Security Council addressed to the Secretary-General

Letter dated 9 October 1992 from the President of the Security Council addressed to the Secretary-General

Letter dated 3 November 1992 from the President of the Security Council addressed to the Secretary-General

Letter dated 11 October 1993 from the President of the Security Council addressed to the Secretary-General

Letter dated 3 December 1993 from the President of the Security Council addressed to the Permanent Representative of Iraq to the United Nations

Letter dated 12 March 1996 from the President of the Security Council addressed to the Executive Chairman of the Special Commission established by the Secretary-General pursuant to paragraph 9 (b)(i) of Security Council Resolution 687 (1991)

Letter dated 20 May 1996 from the Secretary-General addressed to the President of the Security Council

Letter dated 23 May 1996 from the President of the Security Council addressed to the Secretary-General

Letter dated 7 June 1997 from the Secretary-General addressed to the President of the Security Council

Letter dated 4 August 1997 from the Secretary-General addressed to the President of the Security Council

Letter dated 13 November 1997 from the Secretary-General addressed to the President of the Security Council

Letter dated 14 November 1997 from the President of the Security Council addressed to the Executive Chairman of the Special Commision established by the Secretary-General pursuant to paragraph 9 (b)(i) of Security Council Resolution 687 (1991)

Letter dated 5 January 1998 from the Secretary-General addressed to the President of the Security Council

Letter dated 25 February 1998 from the Secretary-General addressed to the President of the Security Council

Letter dated 9 March 1998 from the Secretary-General addressed to the President of the Security Council

Letter dated 15 April 1998 from the Secretary-General addressed to the President of the Security Council

Letter dated 29 May 1998 from the Secretary-General addressed to the President of the Security Council

Letter dated 30 May 1998 from the Secretary-General addressed to the President of the Security Council

Letter dated 11 August 1998 from the Secretary-General addressed to the President of the Security Council

Letter dated 12 August 1998 from the Executive Chairman of the Special Commission established by the Secretary-General pursuant to paragraph 9 (b) (i) of Security Council Resolution 687 (1991) addressed to the President of the Security Council

Letter dated 18 August 1998 from the President of the Security Council addressed to the Director General of the International Atomic Energy Agency

Letter dated 18 August 1998 from the President of the Security Council addressed to the Executive Chairman of the Special Commision established by the Secretary-General pursuant to paragraph 9 (b)(i) of Security Council Resolution 687 (1991)

Letter dated 7 October 1998 from the President of the Security Council addressed to the Secretary-General President of the Security Council

Letter dated 14 November 1998 from the Secretary-General addressed to the President of the Security Council

Letter dated 25 November 1998 from the Secretary-General addressed to the President of the Security Council

Letter dated 15 December 1998 from the Secretary-General addressed to the President of the Security Council

Letter dated 6 April 1999 from the President of the Security Council addressed to the Secretary-General

Letter dated 13 May 1999 from the Secretary-General addressed to the President of the Security Council

Letter dated 24 May 1999 from the Secretary-General addressed to the President of the Security Council

Letter dated 24 May 1999 from the Assistant Secretary-General for Legal Affairs in Charge of the Office of Legal Affairs addressed to the Chargé d'affaires a.i. of the Permanent Mission of Iraq to the United Nations

Letter dated 11 June 1999 from the Secretary-General addressed to the President of the Security Council

Letter dated 2 July 1999 from the Secretary-General addressed to the President of the Security Council

Letter dated 6 October 1999 from the President of the Security Council addressed to the Secretary-General

Letter dated 12 October 1999 from the Secretary-General addressed to the President of the Security Council

Letter dated 22 October 1999 from the Secretary-General addressed to the President of the Security Council

Letter dated 13 December 1999 from the Secretary-General addressed to the President of the Security Council

Letter dated 24 February 2000 from the Secretary-General addressed to the President of the Security Council

Letter dated 1 March 2000 from the President of the Security Council addressed to the Secretary-General

Lettter dated 30 June 2000 from the Secretary-General addressed to the President of the Security Council

Letter dated 10 July 2000 from the President of the Security Council addressed ot the Secretary-General

Letter dated 5 October 2000 from the President of the Security Council addressed to the Secretary-General

AS. 24 The situation of the Kurds in Iraq

Meetings: **1991**: **2982**
1992: 3059

Resolution 688 (1991) 5 April 1991

AS. 25 The Situation in the Republic of Yemen

Meetings: **1994**: **3386, 3394,** 3396

Resolution 924 (1994) of 1 June 1994
Resolution 931 (1994) of 29 June 1994

Statement, 30 June 1994

Letter dated 18 July 1994 from the President of the Security Council addressed to the Secretary-General

AS. 26 The Democratic People's Republic of Korea and the Treaty on Non-Profileration of Nuclear Weapons
Agreed framework of 21 October 1994 between the United States of America and the Democratic People's Republic of Korea

Meetings: **1993**: **3212**
1994: 3357, 3383, 3451

Resolution 825 (1993) of 11 May 1993

Statement, 8 April 1993
Statement, 31 March 1994
Statement, 30 May 1994
Statement, 4 November 1994

AS. 27 Relations between the Republic of Korea and the Democratic People's Republic of Korea
Incident of a submarine of the Democratic People's Republic of Korea

Meetings: **1996**: 3704

Statement, 15 October 1996

AS. 28 The Situation relating to Nagorny-Karabakh

Meetings: **1992**: 3127
1993: 3194, **3205, 3259,** 3264, **3292, 3313**
1995: 3525

Resolution 822 (1993) of 30 April 1993
Resolution 853 (1993) of 29 July 1993
Resolution 874 (1993) of 14 October 1993
Resolution 884 (1993) of 12 November 1993

Statement, 12 May 1992
Statement, 26 August 1992
Statement, 27 October 1992
Statement, 6 April 1993
Statement, 18 August 1993
Statement, 26 April 1995

AS. 29 The situation in Georgia
Reports of the Secretary-General on the United Nations Observer Mission in Georgia (UNOMIG)
Reports of the Secretary-General concerning the sitiuation in Abkhazia, Georgia

Meetings: **1992**: 3121
1993: 3169, 3249, **3252, 3261, 3268,** 3279, **3295, 3304,** 3307, **3325**
1994: **3332, 3345,** 3346, **3354,** 3362, **3398, 3407,** 3476
1995: **3488,** 3509, **3535,** 3567
1996: 3658, **3618, 3680, 3707**
1997: **3735,** 3774, **3807,** 3830
1998: **3851,** 3887, **3912,** 3948
1999: **3972,** 3997, **4029,** 4065
2000: **4094,** 4137, **4179,** 4221

Resolution 849 (1993) of 9 July 1993
Resolution 854 (1993) of 6 August 1993
Resolution 858 (1993) of 24 August 1993
Resolution 876 (1993) of 19 October 1993
Resolution 881 (1993) of 4 November 1993
Resolution 892 (1993) of 22 December 1993
Resolution 896 (1994) of 31 January 1994
Resolution 901 (1994) of 4 March 1994
Resolution 906 (1994) of 25 March 1994
Resolution 934 (1994) of 30 June 1994
Resolution 937 (1994) of 21 July 1994
Resolution 971 (1995) of 12 January 1995
Resolution 993 (1995) of 12 May 1995
Resolution 1036 (1996) of 12 January 1996

Resolution 1065 (1996) of 12 July 1996
Resolution 1077 (1996) of 22 October 1996
Resolution 1096 (1997) of 30 January 1997
Resolution 1124 (1997) of 31 July 1997
Resolution 1150 (1998) of 30 January 1998
Resolution 1187 (1998) of 30 July 1998
Resolution 1225 (1999) of 28 January 1999
Resolution 1255 (1999) of 30 July 1999
Resolution 1287 (2000) of 31 January 2000
Resolution 1311 (2000) of 28 July 2000

Statement, 10 September 1992
Statement, 8 October 1992
Statement, 29 January 1993
Statement, 2 July 1993
Statement, 17 September 1993
Statement, 8 November 1993
Statement, 8 April 1994
Statement, 2 December 1994
Statement, 17 March 1995
Statement, 18 August 1995
Statement, 25 April 1996
Statement, 22 October 1996
Statement, 8 May 1997
Statement, 6 November 1997
Statement, 28 May 1998
Statement, 25 November 1998
Statement, 7 May 1999
Statement, 12 November 1999
Statement, 11 May 2000
Statement, 14 November 2000

Letter dated 16 June 1994 from the President of the Security Council addressed to the Secretary-General

Letter dated 10 July 1998 from the President of the Security Council addressed to the Secretary-General

AS. 30 The situation in Tajikistan and along the Tajik-Afghan border
Reports of the Secretary-General on the United Nations of Observers in Tajikistan (UNMOT)

Meetings: **1992**: 3131
1993: 3266
1994: 3427, 3452, **3482**
1995: 3515, 3539, **3544,** 3570, 3589, **3606**
1996: 3646, 3665, **3673,** 3696, **3724**
1997: 3739, **3752, 3788, 3816, 3833**
1998: 3856, **3879, 3943**
1999: **3981, 4004,** 4034, **4064**
2000: 4115, 4116, 4140, 4141

Resolution 968 (1994) of 16 December 1994
Resolution 999 (1995) of 16 June 1995
Resolution 1030 (1995) of 14 December 1995
Resolution 1061 (1996) of 14 June 1996
Resolution 1089 (1996) of 13 December 1996
Resolution 1099 (1997) of 14 March 1997
Resolution 1113 (1997) of 12 June 1997
Resolution 1128 (1997) of 12 September 1997
Resolution 1138 (1997) of 14 November 19997
Resolution 1167 (1998) of 14 May 1998
Resolution 1206 (1998) of 12 November 1998
Resolution 1240 (1999) of 15 May 1999
Resolution 1274 (1999) of 12 November 1999

Statement, 30 October 1992
Statement, 23 August 1993
Statement, 22 September 1994
Statement, 8 November 1994
Statement, 12 April 1995
Statement, 19 May 1995
Statement, 25 August 1995
Statement, 6 November 1995
Statement, 29 March 1996
Statement, 21 May 1996

Statement, 20 September 1996
Statement, 7 February 1998
Statement, 24 February 1998
Statement, 23 February 1999
Statement, 19 August 1999
Statement, 21 March 2000
Statement ,12 May 2000

Letter dated 23 November 1993 from the President of the Security Council addressed to the Secretary-General

Letter dated 22 April 1994 from the President of the Security Council addressed to the Secretary-General

Letter dated 19 May 1994 from the President of the Security Council addressed to the Secretary-General

Letter dated 29 September 1994 from the President of the Security Council addressed to the Secretary-General

Letter dated 17 October 1997 from the Secretary-General addressed to the President of the Security Council

Letter dated 10 July 1999 from the Secretary-General addressed to the President of the Security Council

Letter dated 14 July 1999 from the Secretary-General addressed to the President of the Security Council

Letter dated 26 July 1999 from the Secretary-General addressed to the President of the Security Council

Letter dated 26 May 2000 from the Secretary-General addressed to the President of the Security Council

Letter dated 1 June 2000 from the President of the Security Council addressed to the Secretary-General

AS. 31 The situation in Timor
The situation in East-Timor
Reports of the Secretary-General on the United Nations Transitional Administration in East Timor
Report of the Security Council Mission to East Timor and Indonesia

Meeting: 1999: **3998, 4013,** 4019, **4031, 4038,** 4041, 4042, 4043, 4043 (Resumption), **4045, 4057,** 4085
2000: 4097, 4114, 4133, 4147, 4165, 4180, 4182, 4191, **4195,** 4198, 4203, 4206, 4227, 4228, 4230, 4236, 4244

Resolution 1236 (1999) of 7 May 1999
Resolution 1246 (1999) of 11 June 1999
Resolution 1257 (1999) of 3 August 1999
Resolution 1262 (1999) of 27 August 1999
Resolution 1264 (1999) of 15 September 1999
Resolution 1272 (1999) of 25 October 1999
Resolution 1319 (2000) of 8 September 2000

Statement, 29 June 1999
Statement, 3 September 1999
Statement, 3 August 2000
Statement, 21 November 2000
Statement, 6 December 2000

Letter dated 10 July 1999 from the Secretary-General addressed to the President of the Security Council

Letter dated 14 July 1999 from the Secretary-General addressed to the President of the Security Council

Letter dated 26 July 1999 from the Secretary-General addressed to the President of the Security Council

Letter dated 28 July 1999 from the Secretary-General addressed to the President of the Security Council

Letter dated 3 September 1999 from the Secretary-General addressed to the President of the Security Council

Letter dated 5 September 1999 from the President of the Security Council addressed to the Secretary-General

Letter dated 6 September 1999 from the President of the Security Council addressed to the Secretary-General

Letter dated 4 October 1999 from the Secretary-General addressed to the President of the Security Council

Letter dated 23 November 1999 from the President of the Security Council addressed to the Secretary-General

Letter dated 31 January 2000 from the Secretary-General addressed to the President of the General Assembly, the President of the Security Council and the Chairperson of the Commision on Human Rights

Letter dated 18 May 2000 from the Secretary-General addressed to the President of the Security Council

Letter dated 18 May 2000 from the President of the Security Council addressed to the Secretary-General

Letter dated 25 October 2000 from the President of the Security Council addressed to the Secretary-General

AS. 32 The Bougainville Conflict (Papua New Guinea)

Meetings: **1998**: 3874

Statement, 22 April 1998

Letter dated 2 June 1998 from the Secretary-General addressed to the President of the Security Council

Letter dated 15 June 1998 from the President of the Security Council addressed to the Secretary-General

Letter dated 20 November 1998 from the Secretary-General addressed to the President of the Security Council

Letter dated 11 December 1998 from the President of the Security Council addressed to the Secretary-General

Letter dated 28 October 1999 from the Secretary-General addressed to the President of the Security Council

Letter dated 10 November 1999 from the President of the Security Council addressed to the Secretary-General

AS. 33 Solomon Islands Peace Agreement

Meetings: **2000**: 4224

Statement, 16 November 2000

6

CENTRAL AND LATIN AMERICA AND THE CARRIBEAN

C.L.A.C. 01 Question submitted by Guatemala

Meetings: **1954**: **675,** 676.

Resolution 104 (1954) of 20 June 1954

C.L.A.C. 02 Question relating to the case of Adolf Eichmann

Meetings: **1960**: 865, 866, 867, **868.**

Resolution 138 (1960) of 23 June 1960

C.L.A.C. 03 Complaint by Cuba against the United States of America (July 1960)

Meetings: **1960**: 874, 875, **876.**

Resolution 144 (1960) of 19 July 1960

K. Wellens (ed.),
Resolutions and Statements of the United Nations Security Council (1946-2000), 107–113.

C.L.A.C. 04 Question relating to the Dominican Republic

Meetings: **1960**: 893, **895.**
1961: 983.

Resolution 156 (1960) of 9 September 1960

C.L.A.C. 05 The situation in the Dominican Republic

Meetings: **1965**: 1196, 1198, 1200, 1202, 1203, 1204, 1207, **1208,** 1209, 1212, 1213, 1214, 1215, 1216, **1217,** 1218, 1219, 1220, 1221, 1222, 1223, 1225, 1226, 1227, 1228, 1229, 1230, 1231, 1232, 1233.

Resolution 203 (1965) of 14 May 1965
Resolution 205 (1965) of 22 May 1965

Decision, 19 May 1965

Statement, 26 July 1965

C.L.A.C. 06 Request of Panama concerning the holding of meetings of the Security Council in Panama City

Meetings: **1973**: 1684, **1686.**

Resolution 325 (1973) of 26 January 1973

C.L.A.C. 07 Consideration of measures for the maintenance and strengthening of international peace and security in Latin America in conformity with the provisions and principles of the Charter

Meetings: **1973**: 1695, 1696, 1697, 1698, 1699, 1700, 1701, 1702, 1703, **1704.**

Resolution 330 (1973) of 21 March 1973

Statement, 21 March 1973

C.L.A.C. 08 Question concerning the situation in the region of the Falkland Islands (Islas Malvinas)

Meetings: **1982**: 2345, 2346, 2349, **2350,** 2360, 2362, 2363, 2364, 2366, **2368,** 2371, 2372, 2373.
1988: 2800, 2801.

Resolution 502 (1982) of 3 April 1982
Resolution 505 (1982) of 26 May 1982

Statement, 1 April 1982
Statement, 5 May 1982

C.L.A.C. 09 Complaint by Nicaragua

Meetings: **1983**: 2431, 2432, 2433, 2434, 2435, 2436, **2437,** 2477.
1985: 2577, 2578, 2579, **2580.**

Resolution 530 (1983) of 19 May 1983
Resolution 562 (1985) of 10 May 1985

C.L.A.C. 10 Central America: efforts towards peace

Meetings: **1989**: **2871, 2890,** 2896, 2897.
1990: **2913, 2919, 2921,** 2922, **2927, 2952.**
1991: **2986, 2988,** 3010, 3016.
1992: **3030, 3031, 3129, 3142**
1993: 3172, 3185, **3223,** 3236, 3306, **3321**
1994: 3360, **3381,** 3425, **3465**
1995: **3528**
1997: 3730, **3732,** 3744, 3780

Resolution 637 (1989) of 27 July 1989
Resolution 644 (1989) of 7 November 1989
Resolution 650 (1989) of 27 March 1990
Resolution 653 (1989) of 20 April 1990
Resolution 654 (1989) of 4 May 1990
Resolution 656 (1990) of 8 June 1990
Resolution 675 (1990) of 5 November 1990
Resolution 691 (1991) of 6 May 1991
Resolution 693 (1991) of 20 May 1991
Resolution 714 (1991) of 30 September 1991
Resolution 719 (1991) of 6 November 1991
Resolution 729 (1992) of 14 January 1992
Resolution 730 (1992) of 16 January 1992
Resolution 784 (1992) of 30 October 1992
Resolution 791 (1992) of 30 November 1992
Resolution 832 (1993) of 27 May 1993
Resolution 888 (1993) of 30 November 1993
Resolution 920 (1994) of 26 May 1994
Resolution 961 (1994) of 23 November 1994
Resolution 991 (1995) of 28 April 1995
Resolution 1094 (1997) of 20 January 1997

Statement, 8 December 1989
Statement, 23 May 1990
Statement, 3 January 1992
Statement, 3 June 1992
Statement, 9 February 1993
Statement, 18 March 1993
Statement, 11 June 1993
Statement, 5 November 1993
Statement, 7 April 1994
Statement, 16 September 1994
Statement, 5 March 1997
Statement, 22 May 1997

Letter dated 12 July 1993 from the President of the Security Council addressed to the Secretary-General

Letter dated 10 December 1993 from the President of the Security Council addressed to the Secretary-General

Letter dated 30 September 1996 from the Secretary-General addressed to the President of the General Assembly and to the President of the Security Council

Letter dated 16 January 1997 from the Secretary-General addressed to the President of the Security Council

Letter dated 5 February 1997 from the Secretary-General addressed to the President of the Security Council

C.L.A.C. 11 Shooting down of two civil aircraft on 24 February 1996
Letter dated 26 February 1996 from the Permanant Representative of the United States of America addressed to the President of the Security Council

Meetings: **1996**: 3634, 3635, **3683**

Resolution 1067 (1996) of 26 July 1996

Statement, 27 February 1996

C.L.A.C. 12 The Question concerning Haiti
Reports of the Secretary-General on the United Nations Mission in Haiti (UNMIH)
Reports of the Secretary-General on the United Nations Assistance Mission in Haiti (UNAMIH)
Reports of the Secretary-General on the United Nations Support Mission in Haiti (UNSMIH)
Reports of the Secretary-General on the United Nations Transition Mission in Haiti (UNTMIH)
Reports of the Secretary-General on the United Nations Civilian Police Mission in Haiti (MIPONUH)

Meetings: **1991**: 3011
1993: **3238, 3271, 3272,** 3278, 3289, 3314, **3282, 3291, 3293,** 3301
1994: 3328, **3352, 3376, 3397,** 3403, **3413,** 3429, **3430, 3437, 3470**
1995: **3496,** 3523, **3559,** 3594
1996: **3638, 3676, 3719, 3721**
1997: **3806, 3837**
1998: 3866, **3949**
1999: **4074**
2000: 4112

Resolution 841 (1993) of 16 June 1993
Resolution 861 (1993) of 27 August 1993
Resolution 862 (1993) of 31 August 1993
Resolution 867 (1993) of 23 September 1993
Resolution 873 (1993) of 13 October 1993
Resolution 875 (1993) of 16 October 1993
Resolution 905 (1994) of 23 March 1994
Resolution 917 (1994) of 6 May 1994
Resolution 933 (1994) of 30 June 1994
Resolution 940 (1994) of 31 July 1994
Resolution 944 (1994) of 29 September
Resolution 948 (1994) of 14 October 1994
Resolution 964 (1994) of 29 November 1994
Resolution 975 (1995) of 30 January 1995
Resolution 1007 (1995) of 31 July 1995
Resolution 1048 (1996) of 29 February 1996
Resolution 1063 (1996) of 28 June 1996
Resolution 1085 (1996) of 29 November 1996
Resolution 1086 (1996) of 5 December 1996
Resolution 1123 (1997) of 30 July 1997
Resolution 1141 (1997) of 28 November 1997
Resolution 1212 (1998) of 25 November 1998
Resolution 1277 (1999) of 30 November 1999

Statement, 17 September 1993
Statement, 11 October 1993
Statement, 25 October 1993
Statement, 30 October 1993

Statement, 15 November 1993
Statement, 10 January 1994
Statement, 11 May 1994
Statement, 14 May 1994
Statement, 12 July 1994
Statement, 30 August 1994
Statement, 24 April 1995
Statement, 16 November 1995
Statement, 25 March 1998
Statement, 15 March 2000

Exchange of Letters between the Secretary-General and the President of the Security Council: Letters dated 7 September 1990 and 9 October 1990

Letter dated 15 July 1993 from the President of the Security Council addressed to the Secretary-General

Letter dated 19 July 1994 from the President of the Security Council addressed to the Secretary-General

7

MIDDLE EAST

PAL The Palestine question

Meetings: **1947**: **222.**

1948: 243, 253, 254, 255, 258, 260, 261, 262, **263,** 267, 269, 270, 271, 274, 275, **277,** 282, **283, 287,** 289, 291, 292, 293, 294, 295, 296, 297, 298, 299, 301, **302,** 303, 305, 306, 307, 308, 309, **310,** 311, 313, 314, 317, 320, 330, **331,** 332, 333, 334, 335, 336, 337, **338,** 339, 340, 343, 349, 352, **354,** 356, **358,** 365, **367,** 373, 374, **375,** 376, **377,** 378, 379, 380, **381,** 394, 395, **396.**

1949: 433, 434, 435, **437.**

1950: 511, 514, 517, 518, 522, **524.**

1951: 541, 542, 544, **545,** 546, **547,** 549, 550, 551, 552, 553, 555, 556, **558.**

1953: 626, 627, 629, 630, **631,** 632, 633, 635, 636, 637, 638, 639, 640, **642,** 643, 645, 646, 648, 649, 650, 651, 652, 653, 654.

1955: 687, 688, 692, 693, 694, **695, 696,** 697, 698, **700,** 707, 709.

1956: 710, 711, 712, 713, 714, **715,** 717, 718, 719, 720, 721, **722,** 723, 724, 725, 726, 727, **728,** 744, 745, 748, 749, 750.

1958: 809, **810,** 841, 844.

1961: 947, 948, **949.**

1962: 999, 1000, 1001, 1002, 1003, 1004, 1005, **1006.**

1966: 1288, 1289, 1290, 1291, 1292, 1293, 1294, 1295, 1305, 1307, 1308, 1309, 1310, 1312, 1313, 1314, 1316, 1317, 1319, 1320, 1321, 1322, 1323, 1324, 1325, 1326, 1327, **1328.**

Resolution 42 (1948) of 5 March 1948
Resolution 43 (1948) of 1 April 1948

K. Wellens (ed.),
Resolutions and Statements of the United Nations Security Council (1946-2000), 115–129.

Resolution 44 (1948) of 1 April 1948
Resolution 46 (1948) of 17 April 1948
Resolution 48 (1948) of 23 April 1948
Resolution 49 (1948) of 22 May 1948
Resolution 50 (1948) of 29 May 1948
Resolution 53 (1948) of 7 July 1948
Resolution 54 (1948) of 15 July 1948
Resolution 56 (1948) of 19 August 1948
Resolution 57 (1948) of 18 September 1948
Resolution 59 (1948) of 19 October 1948
Resolution 60 (1948) of 29 October 1948
Resolution 61 (1948) of 4 November 1948
Resolution 62 (1948) of 16 November 1948
Resolution 66 (1948) of 29 December 1948
Resolution 72 (1949) of 11 August 1949
Resolution 73 (1949) of 11 August 1949
Resolution 89 (1950) of 17 November 1950
Resolution 92 (1951) of 8 May 1951
Resolution 93 (1951) of 18 May 1951
Resolution 95 (1951) of 1 September 1951
Resolution 100 (1953) of 27 October 1953
Resolution 101 (1953) of 24 November 1953
Resolution 106 (1955) of 29 March 1955
Resolution 107 (1955) of 30 March 1955
Resolution 108 (1955) of 8 September 1955
Resolution 111 (1956) of 19 January 1956
Resolution 113 (1956) of 4 April 1956
Resolution 114 (1956) of 4 June 1956
Resolution 127 (1958) of 22 January 1958
Resolution 162 (1961) of 11 April 1961
Resolution 171 (1962) of 9 April 1962
Resolution 228 (1966) of 25 November 1966

Questionnaire, 18 May 1948

Statement, 19 October 1948

M.E. 01 The situation in the Middle East: general

Meetings: **1967**: 1341, 1342, 1343, 1344, 1345, 1346, 1347, **1348,** 1349, **1350,** 1351, **1352,** 1353, 1354, 1355, 1356, **1357,** 1358, 1359, 1360, **1361,** 1365, 1366, 1369, 1370, **1371,** 1373, 1375, 1377, 1379, 1380, 1381, **1382.**

1968: 1401, 1402, 1403, 1404, 1405, 1406, **1407,** 1409, 1410, 1411, 1412, 1416, **1417,** 1418, 1419, **1420,** 1421, 1422, 1423, 1424, 1425, **1426,** 1434, 1435, 1436, 1437, 1438, 1439, **1440,** 1446, 1447, 1448, 1449, 1451, **1452,** 1453, **1454,** 1456, 1457.

1969: 1466, 1467, 1468, 1469, 1470, 1471, 1472, **1473,** 1482, 1483, 1484, **1485,** 1507, 1508, 1509, 1510, 1511, **1512.**

1971: 1579, 1580, 1581, **1582.**

1973: **1710,** 1717, 1718, 1719, 1720, 1721, 1722, 1723, 1724, 1725, 1726, 1728, 1733, 1734, 1735, 1744, 1745, 1746, **1747, 1748,** 1749.

1974: 1799.

1975: 1859, 1860, 1861, 1862.

1978: 2106.

1984: 2519, 2540.

Resolution 233 (1967) of 6 June 1967
Resolution 234 (1967) of 7 June 1967
Resolution 235 (1967) of 9 June 1967
Resolution 236 (1967) of 11 June 1967
Resolution 237 (1967) of 14 June 1967
Resolution 240 (1967) of 25 October 1967
Resolution 242 (1967) of 22 November 1967
Resolution 248 (1968) of 24 March 1968
Resolution 250 (1968) of 27 April 1968
Resolution 251 (1968) of 2 May 1968
Resolution 252 (1968) of 21 May 1968
Resolution 256 (1968) of 16 August 1968
Resolution 258 (1968) of 18 September 1968
Resolution 259 (1968) of 27 September 1968
Resolution 265 (1969) of 1 April 1969
Resolution 267 (1969) of 3 July 1969

Resolution 271 (1969) of 15 September 1969
Resolution 298 (1971) of 25 September 1971
Resolution 331 (1973) of 20 April 1973
Resolution 338 (1973) of 22 October 1973
Resolution 339 (1973) of 23 October 1973

Statement, 9 July 1967
Statement, 4 April 1968
Statement, 8 September 1968
Statement, 14 June 1973

M.E. 02 Arrangements for the Proposed Peace Conference on the Middle East

Meetings: **1973: 1760**

Resolution 344 (1973) of 15 December 1973

Statement, 20 December 1990
Statement, 22 January 1996

Letter 19 December 1973 from the President of the Security Council addressed to the Secretary-General

Letter dated 10 September 1999 from the Secretary-General addressed to the President of the Security Council

Letter dated 9 November 1999 from the Secretary-General addressed to the President of the Security Council

Letter dated 8 December 1999 from the President of the Security Council addressed to the Secretary-General

M.E. 03 The situation in the Middle East: Report of the Secretary-General on the United Nations Disengagement Force (UNDOF)

Meetings: **1974: 1773, 1774, 1809**
1975: 1822, 1856
1976: 1923, 1975
1977: 2010, 2051
1978: 2079, 2101
1979: 2145, 2174
1980: 2224, 2256
1981: 2278, 2311
1982: 2369, 2403
1983: 2445, 2502
1984: 2544, 2563
1985: 2581, 2630
1986: 2687, 2722
1987: 2748, 2769
1988: 2815, 2831
1989: 2862, 2895
1990: 2925, 2964
1991: 2990, 3019
1992: 3081, 3141
1993: 3220, 3320
1994: 3382, 3467
1995: 3541, 3599
1996: 3669, 3715
1997: 3782, 3835
1998: 3885, 3947
1999: 4009, 4071
2000: 4148, 4235

Resolution 350 (1974) of 31 May 1974
Resolution 363 (1974) of 29 November 1974
Resolution 369 (1975) of 28 May 1975
Resolution 381 (1975) of 30 November 1975
Resolution 390 (1976) of 28 May 1976
Resolution 398 (1976) of 30 November 1976
Resolution 408 (1977) of 26 May 1977
Resolution 420 (1977) of 30 November 1977
Resolution 429 (1978) of 31 May 1978
Resolution 441 (1978) of 30 November 1978

Resolution 449 (1979) of 30 May 1979
Resolution 456 (1979) of 30 November 1979
Resolution 470 (1980) of 30 May 1980
Resolution 481 (1980) of 26 November 1980
Resolution 485 (1981) of 22 May 1981
Resolution 493 (1981) of 23 November 1981
Resolution 506 (1982) of 26 May 1982
Resolution 524 (1982) of 29 November 1982
Resolution 531 (1983) of 26 May 1983
Resolution 543 (1983) of 29 November 1983
Resolution 551 (1984) of 30 May 1984
Resolution 557 (1984) of 28 November 1984
Resolution 563 (1985) of 21 May 1985
Resolution 576 (1985) of 21 November 1985
Resolution 584 (1985) of 29 May 1986
Resolution 590 (1986) of 26 November 1986
Resolution 596 (1987) of 29 May 1987
Resolution 603 (1987) of 25 November 1987
Resolution 613 (1988) of 31 May 1988
Resolution 624 (1988) of 30 November 1988
Resolution 633 (1989) of 30 May 1989
Resolution 645 (1989) of 29 November 1989
Resolution 655 (1990) of 31 May 1990
Resolution 679 (1990) of 30 November 1990
Resolution 695 (1991) of 30 May 1991
Resolution 722 (1991) of 29 November 1991
Resolution 756 (1992) of 29 May 1992
Resolution 790 (1992) of 25 November 1992
Resolution 830 (1993) of 26 May 1993
Resolution 887 (1993) of 29 November 1993
Resolution 921 (1994) of 26 May 1994
Resolution 962 (1994) of 29 November 1994
Resolution 996 (1995) of 30 May 1995
Resolution 1024 (1995) of 28 November 1995
Resolution 1057 (1996) of 30 May 1996
Resolution 1081 (1996) of 27 November 1996
Resolution 1109 (1997) of 28 May 1997
Resolution 1139 (1997) of 21 November 1997

Resolution 1169 (1998) of 27 May 1998
Resolution 1211 (1998) of 25 November 1998
Resolution 1243(1999) of 27 May 1999
Resolution 1276 (1999) of 24 November 1999
Resolution 1300 (2000) of 31 May 2000
Resolution 1328 (2000) of 27 November 2000

Statement, 30 November 1976
Statement, 31 May 1978
Statement, 30 November 1978
Statement, 30 November 1979

M.E. 04 The situation in the Middle East: reports of the Secretary-General on the United Nations Emergency Force (II)

Meetings: **1973**: **1750,** 1751, **1752,** 1754, 1755
1974: **1765, 1799**
1975: **1821,** 1832, **1833, 1851**
1976: **1964**
1977: **2035**
1978: **2091**

Resolution 340 (1973) of 25 October 1973
Resolution 341 (1973) of 27 October 1973
Resolution 346 (1974) of 8 April 1974
Resolution 362 (1974) of 23 October 1974
Resolution 368 (1975) of 17 April 1975
Resolution 371 (1975) of 24 July 1975
Resolution 378 (1975) of 23 October 1975
Resolution 396 (1976) of 22 October 1976
Resolution 416 (1977) of 21 October 1977
Resolution 438 (1978) of 23 October 1978

Statement, 2 November 1973

Letter dated 24 July 1979 from the Secretary-General and addressed to the President of the Security Council

M.E. 05 The situation in the Occupied Arab Territories

Meetings: **1976**: 1893, 1916
1979: 2123, 2124, 2125, 2126, 2127, 2128, 2131, **2134,** 2156, 2157, 2158, **2159**
1980: 2199, 2200, 2201, 2202, **2203, 2221,** 2222, 2223, **2226, 2233,** 2234, 2235, 2236, 2238, 2239, 2241, **2242, 2245,** 2259, **2260**
1981: 2316, 2317, 2318, **2319**
1982: 2322, 2323, 2324, 2325, 2326, 2327, 2328, 2329, **2330,** 2334, 2338, 2340, 2344, 2348, 2352, 2353, 2354, 2355, 2356, 2357, 2401
1983: 2412, 2413, 2414, 2438, 2457, 2458, 2459, 2460, 2461
1985: 2604, 2605
1986: 2643, 2644, 2645, 2646, 2647, 2648, 2649, 2650, 2724, 2725, 2726, **2727**
1987: 2770, 2772, 2773, 2774, 2775, 2776, **2777**
1988: **2780, 2781,** 2785, 2786, 2787, 2789, 2790
1989: 2804, 2805, 2806, 2845, 2846, 2847, 2849, 2850, 2863, 2864, 2865, 2866, 2867, **2870, 2883,** 2887, 2888, 2889
1990: 2910, 2911, 2912, 2914, 2915, 2920, 2923, 2926, 2945, 2946, 2947, **2948, 2949,** 2953, 2954, 2957, 2965, 2966, 2967, 2968, **2970,** Part I and II
1991: 2973, 2980, **2989**
1992: **3026,** 3065, **3151**
1994: 3340, 3341, 3342, **3351**
1995: 3505, 3536, 3536 (Resumption 1), 3536 (Resumption 2), 3538
1996: 3652, 3652 (Resumption 1), 3698, 3698 (Resumption 1), **3698 (Resumption 2)**
1997: 3745, 3745(Resumption 1), 3745(Resumption 2), 3747, 3756
1998: 3900, 3900 (Resumption), 3904

Resolution 446 (1979) of 22 March 1979
Resolution 452 (1979) of 20 July 1979
Resolution 465 (1980) of 1 March 1980

Resolution 468 (1980) of 8 May 1980
Resolution 469 (1980) of 20 May 1980
Resolution 471 (1980) of 5 June 1980
Resolution 476 (1980) of 30 June 1980
Resolution 478 (1980) of 20 August 1980
Resolution 484 (1980) of 19 December 1980
Resolution 497 (1981) of 17 December 1981
Resolution 500 (1982) of 28 January 1982
Resolution 592 (1986) of 8 December 1986
Resolution 605 (1987) of 22 December 1987
Resolution 607 (1988) of 5 January 1988
Resolution 608 (1988) of 14 January 1988
Resolution 636 (1989) of 6 July 1989
Resolution 641 (1989) of 30 August 1989
Resolution 672 (1990) of 12 October 1990
Resolution 673 (1990) of 24 October 1990
Resolution 681 (1990) of 20 December 1990
Resolution 694 (1991) of 24 May 1991
Resolution 726 (1992) of 6 January 1992
Resolution 799 (1992) of 18 December 1992
Resolution 904 (1994) of 18 March 1994
Resolution 1073 (1996) of 28 September 1996

Statement, 26 May 1976
Statement, 11 November 1976
Statement, 14 November 1979
Statement, 4 April 1983
Statement, 26 January 1984
Statement, 26 August 1988
Statement, 19 June 1990
Statement, 4 January 1991
Statement, 27 March 1991
Statement, 4 April 1992
Statement, 13 July 1998

Letter dated 6 May 1997 from the President of the General Assembly addressed to the President of the Security Council

Letter dated 16 July 1997 from the President of the General Assembly addressed to the President of the Security Council

M.E. 06 The Situation in the Middle-East
The Situation in Lebanon
Reports of the Secretary-General on the implementation of Security Council Resolutions 425 (1978) and 426 (1978)
Reports of the Secretary-General on the United Nations Interim Force in Lebanon (UNIFIL)

Meetings: **The Situation in Lebanon**: more general
1968: 1460, 1461, **1462**
1969: 1498, 1499, 1500, 1501, 1502, **1504**
1970: **1537,** 1538, 1539, 1540, 1541, **1542, 1551**
1972: 1643, **1644,** 1648, 1649, **1650,** 1651, 1652, **1653,** 1661, 1662
1973: 1705, 1706, 1707, 1708, 1709, **1711,** 1736, 1737, 1738, 1739, **1740**
1974: 1766, 1767, 1768, **1769**
1975: 1859, 1860, 1861, 1862
1978: 2071, 2072, 2073, **2089**
1979: 2144
1981: 2292, **2293**
1982: **2374, 2375,** 2376, 2377, **2380,** 2381, **2382,** 2384, **2385, 2386,** 2387, 2388, **2389,** 2390, 2391, **2392,** 2394, **2395, 2396**
1983: 2475, **2501**
1984: 2514, 2515, 2516, 2519, 2552, 2553, 2554, 2555, 2556
1985: 2568, 2570, 2572, 2573, **2582**
1986: 2640, 2641, 2642, 2705
1988: 2782, 2783, 2784, 2811, 2813, 2814, 2832
1989: 2851, 2858, 2875, 2884, 2891, 2894, 2903
1992: 3053
1996: 3653
2000: 4131, 4146, 4160

Resolution 262 (1968) of 31 December 1968
Resolution 270 (1969) of 26 August 1969
Resolution 279 (1970) of 12 May 1970

Resolution 280 (1970) of 19 May 1970
Resolution 285 (1970) of 5 September 1970
Resolution 313 (1972) of 28 February 1972
Resolution 316 (1972) of 26 June 1972
Resolution 317 (1972) of 21 July 1972
Resolution 332 (1973) of 21 April 1973
Resolution 337 (1973) of 15 August 1973
Resolution 347(1974) of 24 April 1974
Resolution 436 (1978) of 6 October 1978
Resolution 490 (1981) of 21 July 1981
Resolution 508 (1982) of 5 June 1982
Resolution 509 (1982) of 6 June 1982
Resolution 512 (1982) of 19 June 1982
Resolution 513 (1982) of 4 July 1982
Resolution 515 (1982) of 29 July 1982
Resolution 516 (1982) of 1 August 1982
Resolution 517(1982) of 4 August 1982
Resolution 518 (1982) of 12 August 1982
Resolution 520 (1982) of 17 September 1982
Resolution 521 (1982) of 19 September 1982
Resolution 542 (1983) of 23 November 1983
Resolution 564 (1985) of 31 May 1985

Statement, 20 April 2000
Statement, 23 May 2000
Statement, 18 June 2000

Letter dated 6 April 2000 from the Secretary-General addressed to the President of the Security Council

Letter dated 17 April 2000 from the Secretary-General addressed to the President of the Security Council

UNIFIL **1978**: **2074, 2075, 2076, 2085,** 2086, 2106
1979: **2113,** 2141, 2146, 2147, 2148, **2149,** 2164, 2165, **2180**
1980: 2212, 2213, 2214, 2215, 2216, 2217, **2218, 2232, 2258,** 2261
1981: 2265, 2266, **2289, 2320**
1982: 2331, **2332, 2379, 2393, 2400**

1983: **2411, 2456, 2480,** 2495, 2496
1984: **2530, 2559**
1985: **2575, 2623**
1986: **2681, 2699,** 2706, 2707, **2708,** 2719
1987: **2731, 2751, 2788**
1988: **2822**
1989: **2843, 2873**
1990: **2906, 2931**
1991: **2975, 2997**
1992: **3040, 3102**
1993: **3167, 3258**
1994: **3331, 3409**
1995: **3495, 3558**
1996: **3622,** 3653, **3654, 3685**
1997: **3733, 3804**
1998: **3852, 3913**
1999: **3970, 4028**
2000: **4095, 4177**

Resolution 425 (1978) of 19 March 1978
Resolution 426 (1978) of 19 March 1978
Resolution 427 (1978) of 3 May 1978
Resolution 434 (1978) of 18 September 1978
Resolution 444 (1979) of 19 January 1979
Resolution 450 (1979) of 14 June 1979
Resolution 459 (1979) of 19 December 1979
Resolution 467 (1980) of 24 April 1980
Resolution 474 (1980) of 17 June 1980
Resolution 483 (1980) of 17 December 1980
Resolution 488 (1981) of 19 June 1981
Resolution 498 (1981) of 18 December 1981
Resolution 501 (1982) of 25 February 1982
Resolution 511 (1982) of 18 June 1982
Resolution 519 (1982) of 17 August 1982
Resolution 523 (1982) of 18 October 1982
Resolution 529 (1983) of 18 January 1983
Resolution 536 (1983) of 18 July 1983
Resolution 538 (1983) of 18 October 1983

Resolution 549 (1984) of 19 April 1984
Resolution 555 (1984) of 12 October 1984
Resolution 561 (1985) of 17 April 1985
Resolution 575 (1985) of 17 October 1985
Resolution 583 (1986) of 18 April 1986
Resolution 586 (1986) of 18 July 1986
Resolution 587 (1986) of 23 September 1986
Resolution 594 (1987) of 15 January 1987
Resolution 599 (1987) of 31 July 1987
Resolution 609 (1988) of 29 January 1988
Resolution 617 (1988) of 29 July 1988
Resolution 618 (1988) of 29 July 1988
Resolution 630 (1989) of 30 January 1989
Resolution 639 (1989) of 31 July 1989
Resolution 648 (1990) of 31 January 1990
Resolution 659 (1990) of 31 July 1990
Resolution 684 (1991) of 30 January 1991
Resolution 701 (1991) of 31 July 1991
Resolution 734 (1992) of 29 January 1992
Resolution 768 (1992) of 30 July 1992
Resolution 803 (1993) of 30 January 1993
Resolution 852 (1993) of 28 July 1993
Resolution 895 (1994) of 28 January 1994
Resolution 938 (1994) of 28 July 1994
Resolution 974 (1995) of 30 January 1995
Resolution 1006 (1995) of 28 July 1995
Resolution 1039 (1996) of 29 January 1996
Resolution 1052 (1996) of 18 April 1996
Resolution 1068 (1996) of 30 July 1996
Resolution 1095 (1997) of 28 January 1997
Resolution 1122 (1997) of 29 July 1997
Resolution 1151 (1998) of 30 January 1998
Resolution 1188 (1998) of 30 July 1998
Resolution 1223 (1999) of 28 January 1999
Resolution 1254 (1999) of 30 July 1999
Resolution 1288 (2000) of 31 January 2000
Resolution 1310 (2000) of 27 July 2000

Consensus, 19 April 1972

Statement, 8 December 1978
Statement, 19 January 1979
Statement, 26 April 1979
Statement, 26 April 1979
Statement, 18 April 1980
Statement, 19 March 1981
Statement, 25 June 1981
Statement, 17 July 1981
Statement, 22 April 1982
Statement, 4 June 1982
Statement, 3 August 1982
Statement, 11 November 1983
Statement, 3 December 1983
Statement, 24 May 1985
Statement, 6 June 1986
Statement, 5 September 1986
Statement, 31 October 1986
Statement, 2 December 1986
Statement, 13 February 1987
Statement, 19 March 1987
Statement, 31 March 1989
Statement, 24 April 1989
Statement, 31 July 1989
Statement, 15 August 1989
Statement, 20 September 1989
Statement, 7 November 1989
Statement, 22 November 1989
Statement, 27 December 1989
Statement, 31 July 1990
Statement, 30 January 1991
Statement, 31 July 1991
Statement, 29 January 1992
Statement, 19 February 1992
Statement, 30 July 1992
Statement, 28 January 1993
Statement, 30 July 1993

Statement, 28 January 1994
Statement, 28 July 1994
Statement, 30 January 1995
Statement, 28 July 1995
Statement, 29 January 1996
Statement, 30 July 1996
Statement, 28 January 1997
Statement, 29 July 1997
Statement, 30 January 1998
Statement, 30 July 1998
Statement, 28 January 1999
Statement, 30 July 1999
Statement, 28 January 1999
Statement, 30 July 1999
Statement, 31 January 2000

Letter dated 7 May 1996 from the Secretary-General addressed to the President of the Security Council

Letter dated 24 July 2000 from the Secretary-General addressed to the President of the Security Council

M.E. 07 The situation in the Middle East, including the Palestinian question

Meetings: **2000**: 4204, 4204 (Resumption 1), 4204 (Resumption 2), **4205,** 4217, 4218, 4231, 4233, 4234, 4248

Resolution 1322 (2000) of 7 October 2000

PART II

OTHER MATTERS CONSIDERED BY THE SECURITY COUNCIL

01 Provisional Rules of Procedure of the Security Council

Meetings: **1946**: 1, 11, 23, 25, 31, 41, 42, 48, 71, **84**
1947: **138, 197, 222,** 224
1950: 462
1969: **1463**
1974: **1761**
1982: **2410**
1994: 3420, 3426

Resolution 14 (1946) of 16 December 1946
Resolution 26 (1947) of 4 June 1947
Resolution 33 (1947) of 27 August 1947
Resolution 37 (1947) of 9 December 1947
Resolution 263 (1969) of 24 January 1969
Resolution 345 (1974) of 17 January 1974
Resolution 528 (1982) of 21 December 1982

Statement, 24 January 1969
Statement, 12 June 1970
Statement, 21 October 1970
Statement, 29 January 1985
Statement, 26 September 1985
Statement, 25 August 1994
Statement, 16 September 1994

02 Appointment of a rapporteur or conciliator for a situation or dispute brought to the attention of the Security Council

Meetings: **1950**: **472.**

Resolution 81 (1950) of 24 May 1950

03 Procedure concerning the Admission of new Members to the United Nations
Admission of new Members to the United Nations

Meetings: **Procedure concerning the admission of new members to the United Nations**
1946: 41, **42**, 51.

Admission of new members to the United Nations
1946: 18, 51, 52, 54, 56, **57**, 72, 74, 75, 81, 82, **83**
1947: **132, 137,** 152, 154, 161, 168, 178, 186, **190,** 197, 204, 205, 206, 221, 222
1948: 261, **279,** 280, 318, 351, 383, 384, 385, 386
1949: 409, 410, 413, **414,** 423, 427, 428, 429, 430, 431, 439, 440, 441, 442, 443, 444, 445
1950: **503**
1951: 568, 569
1952: 573, 581, 590, 591, 594, 595, 596, 597, 599, 600, 601, 602, 603, 604
1955: 701, 702, 703, 704, **705,** 706, 708
1956: **716, 731, 732, 756**
1957: **775, 786,** 789, 790
1958: **842,** 843
1960: **850, 864, 869, 870, 871, 872, 890, 891, 892, 907, 908,** 911
1961: **968,** 969, 970, **971,** 984, 985, **986**
1962: **1017, 1018, 1020, 1021**
1963: **1034, 1084**
1964: **1160, 1161**
1965: **1190, 1243**
1966: **1287, 1306, 1330**
1967: **1384**
1968: **1414, 1450, 1458**
1970: **1554**
1971: 1565, **1566,** 1574, **1575,** 1577, 1578, **1587,** 1608, **1609**
1972: **1658, 1659, 1660**
1973: 1729, **1730,** 1731, **1732**
1974: 1775, **1776,** 1777, **1778,** 1790, **1791**
1975: 1834, 1835, 1836, 1837, **1838,** 1839, **1841,** 1842, 1843, 1844, 1845, 1846, 1847, **1848,** 1857, **1858**
1976: 1931, 1932, 1951, **1952,** 1955, 1970, 1971, 1972, 1973, **1974,** 1976, **1977**
1977: 2020, **2021,** 2022, 2023, 2024, **2025**
1978: 2083, **2084,** 2104, **2105**
1979: 2166, **2167**
1980: 2197, **2198,** 2243, **2244**

1981: 2290, **2291**, 2301, **2302**, 2307, **2309**
1983: 2478, **2479**
1984: 2517, **2518**
1990: 2917, **2918**, 2935, **2936**
1991: 2998, 2999, 3000, **3001**, **3002**, **3003**, 3006, **3007**
1992: 3032, **3034**, 3035, 3036, 3037, 3038, **3041**, **3042**, **3043**, **3044**, 3045, **3047**, 3048, **3050**, 3051, **3052**, 3054, **3056**, 3073, **3074**, **3076**, 3077, 3078, **3079**, 3090, **3091**
1993: 3155, 3156, **3157**, **3158**, 3195, **3196**, 3215, 3216, **3218**, **3219**, 3250, **3251**
1994: 3468, **3469**
1999: 3995, 3996, **4016**, **4017**, 4024, **4026**
2000: 4093, **4103**, 4214, **4215**

Resolution 6 (1960) of 17 May 1946
Resolution 8 (1960) of 29 August 1946
Resolution 13 (1960) of 12 December 1946
Resolution 24 (1960) of 30 April 1947
Resolution 25 (1960) of 22 May 1947
Resolution 29 (1960) of 21 August 1947
Resolution 45 (1960) of 10 April 1948
Resolution 69 (1960) of 4 March 1949
Resolution 86 (1960) of 26 September 1950
Resolution 109 (1960) of 14 December 1955
Resolution 112 (1960) of 6 February 1956
Resolution 115 (1960) of 20 July 1956
Resolution 116 (1960) of 26 July 1956
Resolution 121 (1960) of 12 December 1956
Resolution 124 (1960) of 7 March 1957
Resolution 125 (1960) of 5 September 1957
Resolution 131 (1960) of 9 December 1958
Resolution 133 (1960) of 26 January 1960
Resolution 136 (1960) of 31 May 1960
Resolution 139 (1960) of 28 June 1960
Resolution 140 (1960) of 29 June 1960
Resolution 141 (1960) of 5 July 1960
Resolution 142 (1960) of 7 July 1960
Resolution 147 (1960) of 23 August 1960
Resolution 148 (1960) of 23 August 1960
Resolution 149 (1960) of 23 August 1960
Resolution 150 (1960) of 23 August 1960

Resolution 151 (1960) of 23 August 1960
Resolution 152 (1960) of 23 August 1960
Resolution 153 (1960) of 23 August 1960
Resolution 154 (1960) of 23 August 1960
Resolution 155 (1960) of 24 August 1960
Resolution 158 (1960) of 28 September 1960
Resolution 159 (1960) of 28 September 1960
Resolution 160 (1960) of 7 October 1960
Resolution 165 1961) of 26 September 1961
Resolution 166 (1961) of 25 October 1961
Resolution 167 (1961) of 25 October 1961
Resolution 170 (1961) of 14 December 1961
Resolution 172 (1962) of 26 July 1962
Resolution 173 (1962) of 26 July 1962
Resolution 174 (1962) of 12 September 1962
Resolution 175 (1962) of 12 September 1962
Resolution 176 (1962) of 4 October 1962
Resolution 177 (1962) of 15 October 1962

Letter dated 7 May 1963 from the President of the Security Council addressed to the President of the General Assembly (Admission Kuwait)

Resolution 184 (1963) of 16 December 1963
Resolution 185 (1963) of 16 December 1963
Resolution 195 (1964) of 9 October 1964
Resolution 196 (1964) of 30 October 1964
Resolution 197 (1964) of 30 October 1964
Resolution 200 (1965) of 15 March 1965
Resolution 212 (1965) of 20 September 1965
Resolution 213 (1965) of 20 September 1965
Resolution 223 (1966) of 21 June 1966
Resolution 224 (1966) of 14 October 1966
Resolution 225 (1966) of 14 October 1966
Resolution 230 (1966) of 7 December 1966
Resolution 243 (1967) of 12 December 1967
Resolution 249 (1968) of 18 April 1968
Resolution 257 (1968) of 11 September 1968
Resolution 260 (1968) of 6 November 1968
Resolution 287 (1970) of 10 October 1970
Resolution 292 (1971) of 10 February 1971
Resolution 296 (1971) of 18 August 1971

Resolution 297 (1971) of 15 September 1971
Resolution 299 (1971) of 30 September 1971
Resolution 304 (1971) of 8 December 1971
Resolution 335 (1973) of 22 June 1973
Resolution 336 (1973) of 18 July 1973
Resolution 351 (1974) of 10 June 1974
Resolution 352 (1974) of 21 June 1974
Resolution 356 (1974) of 12 August 1974
Resolution 372 (1975) of 18 August 1975
Resolution 373 (1975) of 18 August 1975
Resolution 374 (1975) of 18 August 1975
Resolution 375 (1975) of 22 September 1975
Resolution 376 (1975) of 17 October 1975
Resolution 382 (1975) of 1 December 1975
Resolution 394 (1976) of 16 August 1976
Resolution 397 (1976) of 22 November 1976
Resolution 399 (1976) of 1 December 1976
Resolution 412 (1977) of 7 July 1977
Resolution 413 (1977) of 20 July 1977
Resolution 433 (1978) of 17 August 1978
Resolution 442 (1978) of 6 December 1978
Resolution 453 (1979) of 12 September 1979
Resolution 464 (1980) of 19 February 1980
Resolution 477 (1980) of 30 July 1980
Resolution 489 (1981) of 8 July 1981
Resolution 491 (1981) of 23 September 1981
Resolution 492 (1981) of 10 November 1981
Resolution 537 (1983) of 22 September 1983
Resolution 548 (1984) of 24 February 1984
Resolution 652 (1900) of 17 April 1990
Resolution 663 (1990) of 14 August 1990
Resolution 702 (1991) of 8 August 1991
Resolution 703 (1991) of 9 August 1991
Resolution 704 (1991) of 9 August 1991
Resolution 709 (1991) of 12 September 1991
Resolution 710 (1991) of 12 September 1991
Resolution 711 (1991) of 12 September 1991
Resolution 732 (1992) of 23 January 1992
Resolution 735 (1992) of 29 January 1992
Resolution 736 (1992) of 29 January 1992
Resolution 737 (1992) of 29 January 1992

Resolution 738 (1992) of 29 January 1992
Resolution 739 (1992) of 5 February 1992
Resolution 741 (1992) of 7 February 1992
Resolution 742 (1992) of 14 February 1992
Resolution 744 (1992) of 25 February 1992
Resolution 753 (1992) of 18 May 1992
Resolution 754 (1992) of 18 May 1992
Resolution 755 (1992) of 20 May 1992
Resolution 763 (1992) of 6 July 1992
Resolution 800 (1993) of 8 January 1993
Resolution 801 (1993) of 8 January 1993
Resolution 817 (1993) of 7 April 1993
Resolution 828 (1993) of 26 May 1993
Resolution 829 (1993) of 26 May 1993
Resolution 848 (1993) of 8 July 1993
Resolution 963 (1994) of 29 November 1994
Resolution 1248 (1999) of 25 June 1999
Resolution 1249 (1999) of 25 June 1999
Resolution 1253 (1999) of 28 July 1999
Resolution 1290 (2000) of 17 February 2000
Resolution 1326 (2000) of 31 October 2000

Statement, 8 August 1991
Statement, 9 August 1991
Statement, 9 August 1991
Statement, 12 September 1991
Statement, 23 January 1992
Statement, 6 July 1992
Statement, 29 January 1992
Statement, 29 January 1992
Statement, 29 January 1992
Statement, 29 January 1992
Statement, 5 February 1992
Statement, 7 February 1992
Statement, 14 February 1992
Statement, 25 February 1992
Statement, 18 May 1992
Statement, 18 May 1992
Statement, 20 May 1992
Statement, 6 July 1992
Statement, 8 January 1993

Statement, 8 January 1993
Statement, 7 April 1993
Statement, 26 May 1993
Statement, 26 May 1993
Statement, 8 July 1993
Statement, 29 November 1994
Statement, 25 June 1999
Statement, 25 June 1999
Statement, 28 July 1999
Statement, 17 February 2000
Statement, 31 October 2000

04 Adoption of directives to the Military Staff Committee to meet at a given place and date

Meetings: **1946**: 1, **2**, 23
1947: 132
1948: 319

Resolution 1 (1946) of 25 January 1946

05 International Court of Justice
Definition of conditions under which the International Court of Justice shall be open to States not parties to the Statute
Admission of States which are not members of the United Nations to become a party to the Statute
Participation of States Parties to the Statute of the International Court of Justice but not members of the United Nations in amendments to the Statute
Conditions under which a party to the Statute of the Court that is not a member of the United Nations may participate in electing the Members of the Court
Election of Members of the Court by the Security Council and the General Assembly

Definition of conditions under which the International Court of Justice shall be open to States not parties to the Statute

Meetings: **1946**: 50, **76**

Resolution 9 (1946) of 15 October 1946

Admission of States which are not members of the United Nations to become a party to the Statute

Meetings: **1946**: 78, **80**
1949: 423, **432**
1953: 641, **645**
1987: 2753, **2754**

Resolution 11 (1946) of 15 November 1946
Resolution 71 (1949) of 27 July 1949
Resolution 102 (1953) of 3 December 1953
Resolution 103 (1953) of 3 December 1953
Resolution 600 (1987) of 19 October 1987

Participation of States Parties to the Statute of the International Court of Justice but not members of the United Nations in amendments to the Statute

Meetings: **1969**: **1514.**

Resolution 272 (1969) of 23 October 1969

Conditions under which a party to the Statute of the Court that is not a member of the United Nations may participate in electing the Members of the Court

Meetings: **1948**: **360.**

Resolution 58 (1948) of 28 September 1948

Election of Members of the Court by the Security Council and the General Assembly

Meetings: **1946**: 1, 2, 9
1948: 369, 371
1951: **548,** 567
1953: **618,** 644
1954: **677,** 681
1956: **733,** 757, 758, 759
1957: 760, 793, 794
1958: **840**

1959: 849
1960: **864**, 909, 910
1963: 1071, 1072
1965: **1236**, 1262
1966: 1315, 1318
1969: 1515
1972: 1671
1975: 1855
1978: 2093
1980: **2255**
1981: 2262, 2306, **2321**, 2333, 2561
1982: 2333
1985: **2604**, 2632
1987: **2739**, 2752, 2760, 2761, 2762
1989: **2838**, 2854
1990: 2955, 2956
1991: **3005**, 3021.
1993: **3170**, 3209, 3309, 3310, 3311
1994: **3443**
1995: 3493, **3507**, **3510**, 3546, 3552, **3590**
1996: 3636, 3709
1999: 4059, **4075**
2000: 4107

Resolution 94 (1951) of 29 May 1951
Resolution 99 (1953) of 12 August 1953
Resolution 105 (1954) of 28 July 1954
Resolution 117 (1956) of 6 September 1956
Resolution 130 (1958) of 25 November 1958
Resolution 137 (1960) of 31 May 1960
Resolution 208 (1965) of 10 August 1965
Resolution 480 (1980) of 12 November 1980
Resolution 499 (1981) of 21 December 1981
Resolution 570 (1985) of 12 September 1985
Resolution 595 (1987) of 27 March 1987
Resolution 627 (1989) of 9 January 1989
Resolution 708 (1991) of 28 August 1991
Resolution 805 (1993) of 4 February 1993
Resolution 951 (1994) of 21 October 1994
Resolution 979 (1995) of 9 March 1995
Resolution 980 (1995) of 22 March 1995

Resolution 1018 (1995) of 7 November 1995
Resolution 1278 (1999) of 30 November 1999

06 Travelling expenses and subsistence allowances of alternate representatives on certain Security Council Commissions

Meetings: **1949**: 432, 447, **448**

Resolution 75 (1949) of 27 September 1949

07 Future costs of United Nations Military Observers in Indonesia

Meetings: **1949**: 446, 448, **449**.

Resolution 76 (1949) 5 October 1949

08 The general regulation and reduction of armaments and information on the armed forces of the United Nations

Meetings: **1946**: 88.
1947: 90, 92, 93, 95, 98, 99, 102, 103, 104, **105,** 152.
1949: 407, **408,** 449, **450,** 451, **452.**
1950: 461, **462.**
1952: **571.**

Resolution 18 (1947) of 13 February 1947
Resolution 68 (1949) of 10 February 1949
Resolution 77 (1949) of 11 October 1949
Resolution 78 (1949) of 18 October 1949
Resolution 79 (1950) of 17 January 1950
Resolution 97 (1952) of 30 January 1952

Decision, 8 July 1947

09 International control of atomic energy

Meetings: **1946**: 50
1947: 92, 102, 103, 105, 106, 108, 110, 112, 115, **117**, 142, 143, 145, 146
1948: 318, 321, **325**
1949: 445, 446, **447**

Resolution 20 (1947) of 10 March 1947
Resolution 52 (1948) of 22 June 1948
Resolution 74 (1949) of 16 September 1949

10 Trusteeship of strategic areas

Meetings: **1947**: 113, 116, 118, 119, 123, **124**, 220, 222
1948: **320, 324, 327**
1949: **415**
1990: **2972**
1994: **3455**

Resolution 21 (1947) of 2 April 1947
Resolution 70 (1949) of 7 March 1949
Resolution 683 (1990) of 22 December 1990
Resolution 956 (1994) of 10 November 1994

Decision, 18 June 1948

Decision, 7 March 1949

11 Question of reviewing the Charter of the United Nations

Meetings: **1955**: **707**

Resolution 110 (1955) of 16 December 1955

12 Recommendation regarding the appointment of the Secretary-General

Meetings: **1946**: 1, 4, 9
1950: 509, 510, 512, 513, 515, 516
1953: 612, 613, 614, 615, 616, 617
1957: 792
1961: **972**
1962: 1026
1966: 1301, **1311, 1329**
1971: 1618, 1619, **1620**
1976: **1978**
1981: 2303, 2304, 2305, 2310, **2312**
1986: **2714**
1991: **3017**
1996: 3714, **3725**

Resolution 168 (1961) of 3 November 1961
Resolution 227 (1966) of 28 October 1966
Resolution 229 (1966) of 2 December 1966
Resolution 306 (1971) of 21 December 1971
Resolution 400 (1976) of 7 December 1976
Resolution 494 (1981) of 11 December 1981
Resolution 589 (1986) of 10 October 1986
Resolution 720 (1991) of 21 November 1991
Resolution 1090 (1996) of 13 December 1996
Resolution 1091 (1996) of 13 December 1996

Decision, 31 March 1953
Decision, 26 September 1957
Decision, 30 November 1962

Statement, 29 September 1966
Statement, 2 December 1966
Statement by the Secretary-General, 2 December 1966

13 Consideration of the Draft Report of the Security Council to the General Assembly and related matters

Meetings: **1970**: **1552**
1993: 3221, 3294

1994: 3440
1995: 3593
1996: 3711
1997: 3815
1998: 3923
1999: 4040
2000: 4192

Resolution 286 (1970) of 9 September 1970

Statement, 20 June 1972

Presidential Note, 28 September 1984
Presidential Note, 30 June 1993
Presidential Note, 27 July 1993
Presidential Note, 31 August 1993
Presidential Note, 29 November 1993
Presidential Note, 18 October 1994
Presidential Note, 13 November 1995
Presidential Note, 12 September 1997
Presidential Note, 9 September 1998
Presidential Note, 25 September 1999
Presidential Note, 31 August 2000

14 Security Council methods and procedure
Consideration of the report of the Secretary-General on the work of the organization

Meetings: **1994**: 3483

Statement, 25 August 1994
Statement, 16 December 1994

Presidential Note, 28 February 1994
Presidential Note, 28 July 1994
Presidential Note, 24 January 1996
Presidential Note, 22 August 1996
Presidential Note, 29 August 1996
Presidential Note, 12 June 1997
Presidential Note, 30 April 1998

Presidential Note, 30 October 1998
Presidential Note, 5 January 1999
Presidential Note, 29 January 1999
Presidential Note, 17 February 1999
Presidential Note, 30 December 1999
Presidential Note, 28 February 2000
Presidential Note, 31 March 2000

15 Provisional Rules of Procedure of the Security Council

Meetings: **1994**: 3420, 3426

Statement, 25 August 1994
Statement, 16 September 1994

PART III

CHRONOLOGICAL AND ANALYTICAL LIST OF RESOLUTIONS

Resolution No.	Date			Code
1	25	January	1946	04
2	30	January	1946	AS. 01
3	4	April	1946	AS. 01
4	29	April	1946	W.E. 01
5	8	May	1946	AS. 01
6	17	May	1946	03
7	26	June	1946	W.E. 01
8	29	August	1946	03
9	15	October	1946	05
10	4	November	1946	W.E. 01
11	15	November	1946	05
12	10	December	1946	W.E. 02
13	12	December	1946	03
14	16	December	1946	01
15	19	December	1946	W.E. 02
16	10	January	1947	W.E. 03
17	10	February	1947	W.E. 02
18	13	February	1947	08
19	27	February	1947	C.E.E. 01
20	10	March	1947	09
21	2	April	1947	10
22	9	April	1947	C.E.E. 01
23	18	April	1947	W.E. 02
24	30	April	1947	03
25	22	May	1947	03
26	4	June	1947	01
27	1	August	1947	AS. 02
28	6	August	1947	W.E. 02
29	12	August	1947	03
30	25	August	1947	AS. 02
31	25	August	1947	AS. 02
32	26	August	1947	AS. 02
33	27	August	1947	01
34	15	September	1947	W.E. 02
35	3	October	1947	AS. 02
36	1	November	1947	AS. 02
37	9	December	1947	01

Resolution No.	Date			Code
38	17	January	1948	AS. 11
39	20	January	1948	AS. 11
40	28	February	1948	AS. 02
41	28	February	1948	AS. 02
42	5	March	1948	PAL.
43	1	April	1948	PAL.
44	1	April	1948	PAL.
45	10	April	1948	03
46	17	April	1948	PAL.
47	21	April	1948	AS. 11
48	23	April	1948	PAL.
49	22	May	1948	PAL.
50	29	May	1948	PAL.
51	3	June	1948	AS. 11
52	22	June	1948	09
53	7	July	1948	PAL.
54	15	July	1948	PAL.
55	29	July	1948	AS. 02
56	19	August	1948	PAL.
57	18	September	1948	PAL.
58	28	September	1948	05
59	19	October	1948	PAL.
60	29	October	1948	PAL.
61	4	November	1948	PAL.
62	16	November	1948	PAL.
63	24	December	1948	AS. 02
64	28	December	1948	AS. 02
65	28	December	1948	AS. 02
66	29	December	1948	PAL.
67	28	January	1949	AS. 02
68	10	February	1949	08
69	4	March	1949	03
70	7	March	1949	10
71	27	July	1949	05
72	11	August	1949	PAL.
73	11	August	1949	PAL.
74	16	September	1949	09

Resolution No.	Date			Code
75	27	September	1949	07
76	5	October	1949	07
77	11	October	1949	08
78	18	October	1949	08
79	17	January	1950	08
80	14	March	1950	AS. 11
81	24	May	1950	02
82	25	June	1950	AS. 03
83	27	June	1950	AS. 03
84	7	July	1950	AS. 03
85	31	July	1950	AS. 03
86	26	September	1950	03
87	29	September	1950	AS. 04
88	8	November	1950	AS. 03
89	17	November	1950	PAL.
90	31	January	1951	AS. 03
91	30	March	1951	AS. 11
92	8	May	1951	PAL.
93	18	May	1951	PAL.
94	29	May	1951	05
95	1	September	1951	PAL.
96	10	November	1951	AS. 11
97	20	January	1952	08
98	23	December	1952	AS. 11
99	12	August	1953	05
100	27	October	1953	PAL.
101	24	November	1953	PAL.
102	3	December	1953	05
103	3	December	1953	05
104	20	June	1954	C.L.A.C. 01
105	28	July	1954	05

Resolution No.	Date			Code
106	29	March	1955	PAL.
107	30	March	1955	PAL.
108	8	September	1955	PAL.
109	14	December	1955	03
110	16	December	1955	11
111	19	January	1956	PAL.
112	6	February	1956	03
113	4	April	1956	PAL.
114	4	June	1956	PAL.
115	20	July	1956	03
116	26	July	1956	03
117	6	September	1956	05
118	13	October	1956	W.E. 04
119	31	October	1956	W.E. 04
120	4	November	1956	C.E.E. 02
121	12	December	1956	03
122	24	January	1957	AS. 11
123	21	February	1957	AS. 11
124	7	March	1957	03
125	5	September	1957	03
126	2	December	1957	AS. 11
127	22	January	1958	PAL.
128	11	June	1958	AF. 01
129	7	August	1958	AF. 01
130	25	November	1958	05
131	9	December	1958	03
132	7	September	1959	AS. 05
133	26	January	1960	03
134	1	April	1960	AF. 26
135	27	May	1960	G. 01
136	31	May	1960	03
137	31	May	1960	05
138	23	June	1960	C.L.A.C. 02

Resolution No.	Date			Code
139	28	June	1960	03
140	29	June	1960	03
141	5	July	1960	03
142	7	July	1960	03
143	14	July	1960	AF. 02
144	19	July	1960	C.L.A.C. 03
145	22	July	1960	AF. 02
146	9	August	1960	AF. 02
147	23	August	1960	03
148	23	August	1960	03
149	23	August	1960	03
150	23	August	1960	03
151	23	August	1960	03
152	23	August	1960	03
153	23	August	1960	03
154	23	August	1960	03
155	24	August	1960	03
156	9	September	1960	C.L.A.C. 04
157	17	September	1960	AF. 02
158	28	September	1960	03
159	28	September	1960	03
160	7	October	1960	03
161	21	February	1961	AF. 02
162	11	April	1961	PAL.
163	9	June	1961	AF. 10
164	22	July	1961	AF. 03
165	26	September	1961	03
166	25	October	1961	03
167	25	October	1961	03
168	3	November	1961	12
169	24	November	1961	AF. 02
170	14	December	1961	03
171	9	April	1962	PAL.
172	26	July	1962	03
173	26	July	1962	03
174	12	September	1962	03

Resolution No.	Date			Code
175	12	September	1962	03
176	4	October	1962	03
177	15	October	1962	03
178	24	April	1963	AF. 11
179	11	June	1963	AS. 06
180	31	July	1963	AF. 12
181	7	August	1963	AF. 27
182	4	December	1963	AF. 27
183	11	December	1963	AF. 12
184	16	December	1963	03
185	16	December	1963	03
186	4	March	1964	AS. 08
187	13	March	1964	AS. 08
188	9	April	1964	AS. 07
189	4	June	1964	AS. 09
190	9	June	1964	AF. 27
191	18	June	1964	AF. 27
192	20	June	1964	AS. 08
193	9	December	1964	AS. 08
194	25	September	1964	AS. 08
195	9	October	1964	03
196	30	October	1964	03
197	30	October	1964	03
198	18	December	1964	AS. 08
199	30	December	1964	AF. 04
200	15	March	1965	03
201	19	March	1965	AS. 08
202	6	May	1965	AF. 14
203	14	May	1965	C.L.A.C. 05
204	19	May	1965	AF. 11
205	22	May	1965	C.L.A.C. 05
206	15	June	1965	AS. 08
207	10	August	1965	AS. 08
208	10	August	1965	05
209	4	September	1965	AS. 11

Resolution No.	Date			Code
210	6	September	1965	AS. 11
211	20	September	1965	AS. 11
212	20	September	1965	03
213	20	September	1965	03
214	27	September	1965	AS. 11
215	5	November	1965	AS. 11
216	12	November	1965	AF. 14
217	20	November	1965	AF. 14
218	23	November	1965	AF. 12
219	17	December	1965	AS. 08
220	16	March	1966	AS. 08
221	9	April	1966	AF. 14
222	16	June	1966	AS. 08
223	21	June	1966	03
224	14	October	1966	03
225	14	October	1966	03
226	14	October	1966	AF. 04
227	28	October	1966	12
228	25	November	1966	PAL.
229	2	December	1966	12
230	7	December	1966	03
231	15	December	1966	AS. 08
232	16	December	1966	AF. 14
233	6	June	1967	M.E. 01
234	7	June	1967	M.E. 01
235	9	June	1967	M.E. 01
236	11	June	1967	M.E. 01
237	14	June	1967	M.E. 01
238	19	June	1967	AS. 08
239	10	July	1967	AF. 04
240	25	October	1967	M.E. 01
241	15	November	1967	AF. 04
242	22	November	1967	M.E. 01
243	12	December	1967	03
244	22	December	1967	AS. 08

Resolution No.	Date			Code
245	25	January	1968	AF. 31
246	14	March	1968	AF. 31
247	18	March	1968	AS. 08
248	24	March	1968	M.E. 01
249	18	April	1968	03
250	27	April	1968	M.E. 01
251	2	May	1968	M.E. 01
252	21	May	1968	M.E. 01
253	29	May	1968	AF. 14
254	18	June	1968	AS. 08
255	19	June	1968	G. 02
256	16	August	1968	M.E. 01
257	11	September	1968	03
258	18	September	1968	M.E. 01
259	27	September	1968	M.E. 01
260	6	November	1968	03
261	10	December	1968	AS. 08
262	31	December	1968	M.E. 06
263	24	January	1969	01
264	20	March	1969	AF. 31
265	1	April	1969	M.E. 01
266	10	June	1969	AS. 08
267	3	July	1969	M.E. 01
268	28	July	1969	AF. 18
269	12	August	1969	AF. 31
270	26	August	1969	M.E. 06
271	15	September	1969	M.E. 01
272	23	October	1969	05
273	9	December	1969	AF. 11
274	11	December	1969	AS. 08
275	22	December	1969	AF. 13
276	30	January	1970	AF. 31
277	18	March	1970	AF. 14
278	11	May	1970	AS. 10
279	12	May	1970	M.E. 06
280	19	May	1970	M.E. 06

Resolution No.	Date			Code
281	9	June	1970	AS. 08
282	23	July	1970	AF. 28
283	29	July	1970	AF. 31
284	29	July	1970	AF. 31
285	5	September	1970	M.E. 06
286	9	September	1970	13
287	10	October	1970	03
288	17	November	1970	AF. 14
289	23	November	1970	AF. 13
290	8	December	1970	AF. 13
291	10	December	1970	AS. 08
292	10	February	1971	03
293	26	May	1971	AS. 08
294	15	July	1971	AF. 11
295	3	August	1971	AF. 13
296	18	August	1971	03
297	15	September	1971	03
298	25	September	1971	M.E. 01
299	30	September	1971	03
300	12	October	1971	AF. 19
301	20	October	1971	AF. 31
302	24	November	1971	AF. 11
303	6	December	1971	AS. 12
304	8	December	1971	03
305	13	December	1971	AS. 08
306	21	December	1971	12
307	21	December	1971	AS. 12
308	19	January	1972	AF. 05
309	4	February	1972	AF. 31
310	4	February	1972	AF. 31
311	4	February	1972	AF. 28
312	4	February	1972	AF. 12
313	28	February	1972	M.E. 06
314	28	February	1972	AF. 14
315	15	June	1972	AS. 08
316	26	June	1972	M.E. 06

Resolution No.	Date			Code
317	21	July	1972	M.E. 06
318	28	July	1972	AF. 14
319	1	August	1972	AF. 31
320	29	September	1972	AF. 14
321	23	October	1972	AF. 11
322	22	November	1972	AF. 12
323	6	December	1972	AF. 31
324	12	December	1972	AS. 08
325	26	January	1973	C.L.A.C. 06
326	2	February	1973	AF. 20
327	2	February	1973	AF. 20
328	10	March	1973	AF. 20
329	10	March	1973	AF. 20
330	21	March	1973	C.L.A.C. 07
331	20	April	1973	M.E. 01
332	21	April	1973	M.E. 06
333	22	May	1973	AF. 14
334	15	June	1973	AS. 08
335	22	June	1973	03
336	18	July	1973	03
337	15	August	1973	M.E. 06
338	22	October	1973	M.E. 01
339	23	October	1973	M.E. 01
340	25	October	1973	M.E. 04
341	27	October	1973	M.E. 04
342	11	December	1973	AF. 31
343	14	December	1973	AS. 08
344	15	December	1973	M.E. 02
345	17	January	1974	01
346	8	April	1974	M.E. 04
347	24	April	1974	M.E. 04
348	28	May	1974	AS. 14
349	29	May	1974	AS. 08
350	31	May	1974	M.E. 03
351	10	June	1974	03
352	21	June	1974	03

Resolution No.	Date			Code
353	20	July	1974	AS. 08
354	23	July	1974	AS. 08
355	1	August	1974	AS. 08
356	12	August	1974	03
357	14	August	1974	AS. 08
358	15	August	1974	AS. 08
359	15	August	1974	AS. 08
360	16	August	1974	AS. 08
361	30	August	1974	AS. 08
362	23	October	1974	M.E. 04
363	29	November	1974	M.E. 03
364	13	December	1974	AS. 08
365	13	December	1974	AS. 08
366	17	December	1974	AF. 31
367	12	March	1975	AS. 08
368	17	April	1975	M.E. 04
369	28	May	1975	M.E. 03
370	13	June	1975	AS. 08
371	24	July	1975	M.E. 04
372	18	August	1975	03
373	18	August	1975	03
374	18	August	1975	03
375	22	September	1975	03
376	17	October	1975	03
377	22	October	1975	AF. 06
378	23	October	1975	M.E. 04
379	2	November	1975	AF. 06
380	6	November	1975	AF. 06
381	30	November	1975	M.E. 03
382	1	December	1975	03
383	13	December	1975	AS. 08
384	22	December	1975	AS. 13
385	30	January	1976	AF. 31
386	17	March	1976	AF. 15
387	31	March	1976	AF. 21
388	6	April	1976	AF. 14

Resolution No.	Date			Code
389	22	April	1976	AS. 13
390	28	May	1976	M.E. 03
391	15	June	1976	AS. 08
392	19	June	1976	AF. 29
393	30	July	1976	AF. 19
394	16	August	1976	03
395	25	August	1976	W.E. 05
396	22	October	1976	M.E. 04
397	22	November	1976	03
398	30	November	1976	M.E. 03
399	1	December	1976	03
400	7	December	1976	12
401	14	December	1976	AS. 08
402	22	December	1976	AF. 22
403	14	January	1977	AF. 17
404	8	February	1977	AF. 07
405	14	April	1977	AF. 07
406	25	May	1977	AF. 17
407	25	May	1977	AF. 22
408	26	May	1977	M.E. 03
409	27	May	1977	AF. 14
410	15	June	1977	AS. 08
411	30	June	1977	AF. 16
412	7	July	1977	03
413	20	July	1977	03
414	15	September	1977	AS. 08
415	29	September	1977	AF. 14
416	21	October	1977	M.E. 04
417	31	October	1977	AF. 30
418	4	November	1977	AF. 30
419	24	November	1977	AF. 07
420	30	November	1977	M.E. 03
421	9	December	1977	AF. 30
422	15	December	1977	AS. 08
423	14	March	1978	AF. 14
424	17	March	1978	AF. 20

Resolution No.	Date			Code
425	19	March	1978	M.E. 06
426	19	March	1978	M.E. 06
427	3	May	1978	M.E. 06
428	6	May	1978	AF. 23
429	31	May	1978	M.E. 03
430	16	June	1978	AS. 08
431	27	July	1978	AF. 31
432	27	July	1978	AF. 31
433	17	August	1978	03
434	18	September	1978	M.E. 06
435	29	September	1978	AF. 31
436	6	October	1978	M.E. 06
437	10	October	1978	AF. 14
438	23	October	1978	M.E. 04
439	13	November	1978	AF. 31
440	27	November	1978	AS. 08
441	30	November	1978	M.E. 03
442	6	December	1978	03
443	14	December	1978	AS. 08
444	19	January	1979	M.E. 06
445	8	March	1979	AF. 14
446	22	March	1979	M.E. 05
447	28	March	1979	AF. 23
448	30	April	1979	AF. 14
449	30	May	1979	M.E. 03
450	14	June	1979	M.E. 06
451	15	June	1979	AS. 08
452	20	July	1979	M.E. 05
453	12	September	1979	03
454	2	November	1979	AF. 23
455	23	November	1979	AF. 20
456	30	November	1979	M.E. 03
457	4	December	1979	AS. 18
458	14	December	1979	AS. 08
459	19	December	1979	M.E. 06
460	21	December	1979	AF. 14
461	31	December	1979	AS. 18

Resolution No.	Date			Code
462	9	January	1980	AS. 19
463	2	February	1980	AF. 14
464	19	February	1980	03
465	1	March	1980	M.E. 05
466	11	April	1980	AF. 19
467	24	April	1980	M.E. 06
468	8	May	1980	M.E. 05
469	20	May	1980	M.E. 05
470	30	May	1980	M.E. 03
471	5	June	1980	M.E. 05
472	13	June	1980	AS. 08
473	13	June	1980	AF. 30
474	17	June	1980	M.E. 06
475	27	June	1980	AF. 23
476	30	June	1980	M.E. 05
477	30	July	1980	03
478	20	August	1980	M.E. 05
479	28	September	1980	AS. 16
480	12	November	1980	05
481	26	November	1980	M.E. 03
482	11	December	1980	AS. 08
483	17	December	1980	M.E. 06
484	19	December	1980	M.E. 05
485	22	May	1981	M.E. 03
486	4	June	1981	AS. 08
487	19	June	1981	AS. 15
488	19	June	1981	M.E. 06
489	8	July	1981	03
490	21	July	1981	M.E. 06
491	23	September	1981	03
492	10	November	1981	03
493	23	November	1981	M.E. 03
494	11	December	1981	12
495	14	December	1981	AS. 08
496	15	December	1981	AS. 20
497	17	December	1981	M.E. 05

Resolution No.	Date			Code
498	18	December	1981	M.E. 06
499	21	December	1981	05
500	28	January	1982	M.E. 05
501	25	February	1982	M.E. 06
502	3	April	1982	C.L.A.C. 08
503	9	April	1982	AF. 30
504	30	April	1982	AF. 08
505	26	May	1982	C.L.A.C. 08
506	26	May	1982	M.E. 03
507	28	May	1982	AS. 20
508	5	June	1982	M.E. 06
509	6	June	1982	M.E. 06
510	15	June	1982	AS. 08
511	18	June	1982	M.E. 06
512	19	June	1982	M.E. 06
513	4	July	1982	M.E. 06
514	12	July	1982	AS. 16
515	29	July	1982	M.E. 06
516	1	August	1982	M.E. 06
517	4	August	1982	M.E. 06
518	12	August	1982	M.E. 06
519	17	August	1982	M.E. 06
520	17	September	1982	M.E. 06
521	19	September	1982	M.E. 06
522	4	October	1982	AS. 16
523	18	October	1982	M.E. 06
524	29	November	1982	M.E. 03
525	7	December	1982	AF. 30
526	14	December	1982	AS. 08
527	15	December	1982	AF. 22
528	21	December	1982	01
529	18	January	1983	M.E. 06
530	19	May	1983	C.L.A.C. 09
531	26	May	1983	M.E. 03
532	31	May	1983	AF. 31
533	7	June	1983	AF. 30

Resolution No.	Date			Code
534	15	June	1983	AS. 08
535	29	June	1983	AF. 22
536	18	July	1983	M.E. 06
537	22	September	1983	03
538	18	October	1983	M.E. 06
539	28	October	1983	AF. 31
540	31	October	1983	AS. 16
541	18	November	1983	AS. 08
542	23	November	1983	M.E. 06
543	29	November	1983	M.E. 03
544	15	December	1983	AS. 08
545	20	December	1983	AF. 23
546	6	January	1984	AF. 23
547	13	January	1984	AF. 30
548	24	February	1984	03
549	19	April	1984	M.E. 06
550	11	May	1984	AS. 08
551	30	May	1984	M.E. 03
552	1	June	1984	AS. 17
553	15	June	1984	AS. 08
554	17	August	1984	AF. 30
555	12	October	1984	M.E. 06
556	23	October	1984	AF. 30
557	28	November	1984	M.E. 03
558	13	December	1984	AF. 30
559	14	December	1984	AS. 08
560	12	March	1985	AF. 30
561	17	April	1985	M.E. 06
562	10	May	1985	C.L.A.C. 09
563	21	May	1985	M.E. 03
564	31	May	1985	M.E. 06
565	14	June	1985	AS. 08
566	19	June	1985	AF. 31
567	20	June	1985	AF. 23
568	21	June	1985	AF. 24

Resolution No.	Date			Code
569	26	July	1985	AF. 30
570	12	September	1985	05
571	20	September	1985	AF. 23
572	30	September	1985	AF. 24
573	4	October	1985	AF. 09
574	7	October	1985	AF. 23
575	17	October	1985	M.E. 06
576	21	November	1985	M.E. 03
577	6	December	1985	AF. 23
578	12	December	1985	AS. 08
579	18	December	1985	G. 03
580	30	December	1985	AF. 22
581	13	February	1986	AF. 25
582	24	February	1986	AS. 16
583	18	April	1986	M.E. 06
584	29	May	1986	M.E. 03
585	13	June	1986	AS. 08
586	18	July	1986	M.E. 06
587	23	September	1986	M.E. 06
588	8	October	1986	AS. 16
589	10	October	1986	12
590	26	November	1986	M.E. 03
591	28	November	1986	AF. 30
592	8	December	1986	M.E. 05
593	11	December	1986	AS. 08
594	15	January	1987	M.E. 06
595	27	March	1987	05
596	29	May	1987	M.E. 03
597	12	June	1987	AS. 08
598	20	July	1987	AS. 16
599	31	July	1987	M.E. 06
600	19	October	1987	05
601	30	October	1987	AF. 31
602	25	November	1987	AF. 23
603	25	November	1987	M.E. 03
604	14	December	1987	AS. 08

Resolution No.	Date			Code
605	22	December	1987	MO. 05
606	23	December	1987	AF. 23
607	5	January	1988	M.E. 05
608	14	January	1988	M.E. 05
609	29	January	1988	M.E. 06
610	16	March	1988	AF. 30
611	25	April	1988	AF. 32
612	9	May	1988	AS. 16
613	31	May	1988	M.E. 03
614	15	June	1988	AS. 08
615	17	June	1988	AF. 30
616	20	July	1988	AS. 21
617	29	July	1988	M.E. 06
618	29	July	1988	M.E. 06
619	9	August	1988	AS. 16
620	26	August	1988	AS. 16
621	20	September	1988	AF. 06
622	31	October	1988	AS. 19
623	23	November	1988	AF. 30
624	30	November	1988	M.E. 03
625	15	December	1988	AS. 08
626	20	December	1988	AF. 33
627	9	January	1989	05
628	16	January	1989	AF. 31
629	16	January	1989	AF. 31
630	30	January	1989	M.E. 06
631	8	February	1989	AS. 16
632	16	February	1989	AF. 31
633	30	May	1989	M.E. 03
634	9	June	1989	AS. 08
635	14	June	1989	G. 04
636	6	July	1989	M.E. 05
637	27	July	1989	C.L.A.C. 10
638	31	July	1989	G. 03
639	31	July	1989	M.E. 06
640	29	August	1989	AF. 31
641	30	August	1989	M.E. 05

Resolution No.	Date			Code
642	29	September	1989	AS. 16
643	31	October	1989	AF. 31
644	7	November	1989	C.L.A.C. 10
645	20	November	1989	M.E. 03
646	14	December	1989	AS. 08
647	11	January	1990	AS. 19
648	31	January	1990	M.E. 06
649	12	March	1990	AS. 08
650	27	March	1990	C.L.A.C. 10
651	29	March	1990	AS. 16
652	17	April	1990	03
653	20	April	1990	C.L.A.C. 10
654	4	May	1990	C.L.A.C. 10
655	31	May	1990	M.E. 03
656	8	June	1990	C.L.A.C. 10
657	15	June	1990	AS. 08
658	27	June	1990	AF. 06
659	31	July	1990	M.E. 06
660	2	August	1990	AS. 23
661	6	August	1990	AS. 23
662	9	August	1990	AS. 23
663	14	August	1990	03
664	18	August	1990	AS. 23
665	25	August	1990	AS. 23
666	13	September	1990	AS. 23
667	16	September	1990	AS. 23
668	20	September	1990	AS. 22
669	24	September	1990	AS. 23
670	25	September	1990	AS. 23
671	27	September	1990	AS. 16
672	12	October	1990	M.E. 05
673	24	October	1990	M.E. 05
674	29	October	1990	AS. 23
675	5	November	1990	C.L.A.C. 10
676	28	November	1990	AS. 16
677	28	November	1990	AS. 23
678	29	November	1990	AS. 23

Resolution No.	Date			Code
679	30	November	1990	M.E. 03
680	14	December	1990	AS. 08
681	20	December	1990	M.E. 05
682	21	December	1990	AS. 08
683	22	December	1990	10
684	30	January	1991	M.E. 06
685	31	January	1991	AS. 16
686	2	March	1991	AS. 23
687	3	April	1991	AS. 23
688	5	April	1991	AS. 24
689	9	April	1991	AS. 23
690	29	April	1991	AF. 06
691	6	May	1991	C.L.A.C. 10
692	20	May	1991	AS. 23
693	20	May	1991	C.L.A.C. 10
694	24	May	1991	M.E. 05
695	30	May	1991	M.E. 03
696	30	May	1991	AF. 34
697	14	June	1991	AS. 08
698	14	June	1991	AS. 08
699	17	June	1991	AS. 23
700	17	June	1991	AS. 23
701	31	July	1991	M.E. 06
702	8	August	1991	03
703	9	August	1991	03
704	9	August	1991	03
705	15	August	1991	AS. 23
706	15	August	1991	AS. 23
707	15	August	1991	AS. 23
708	28	August	1991	05
709	12	September	1991	03
710	12	September	1991	03
711	12	September	1991	03
712	19	September	1991	AS. 23
713	25	September	1991	C.E.E. 03
714	30	September	1991	C.L.A.C. 10
715	11	October	1991	AS. 23

Resolution No.	Date			Code
716	11	October	1991	AS. 08
717	16	October	1991	AS. 22
718	31	October	1991	AS. 22
719	6	November	1991	C.L.A.C. 10
720	21	November	1991	12
721	27	November	1991	C.E.E. 03
722	29	November	1991	M.E. 03
723	12	December	1991	AS. 08
724	15	December	1991	C.E.E. 03
725	31	December	1991	AF. 06
726	6	January	1992	M.E. 05
727	8	January	1992	C.E.E. 03
728	8	January	1992	AS. 22
729	14	January	1992	C.L.A.C. 10
730	16	January	1992	C.L.A.C. 10
731	21	January	1992	AF. 35
732	23	January	1992	03
733	23	January	1992	AF. 36
734	29	January	1992	M.E. 06
735	29	January	1992	03
736	29	January	1992	03
737	29	January	1992	03
738	29	January	1992	03
739	5	February	1992	03
740	7	February	1992	C.E.E. 03
741	7	February	1992	03
742	14	February	1992	03
743	21	February	1992	C.E.E. 03
744	25	February	1992	03
745	28	February	1992	AS. 22
746	17	March	1992	AF. 36
747	24	March	1992	AF. 34
748	31	March	1992	AF. 35
749	7	April	1992	C.E.E. 03
750	10	April	1992	AS. 08
751	24	April	1992	AF. 36
752	15	May	1992	C.E.E. 03

Resolution No.	Date			Code
753	18	May	1992	03
754	18	May	1992	03
755	20	May	1992	03
756	29	May	1992	M.E. 03
757	30	May	1992	C.E.E. 03
758	8	June	1992	C.E.E. 03
759	12	June	1992	AS. 08
760	18	June	1992	C.E.E.03
761	29	June	1992	C.E.E.03
762	30	June	1992	C.E.E.03
763	6	June	1992	03
764	13	July	1992	C.E.E.03
765	16	July	1992	AF.30
766	21	July	1992	AS.22
767	27	July	1992	AF.36
768	30	July	1992	ME.06
769	7	August	1992	C.E.E.03
770	13	August	1992	C.E.E.03
771	13	August	1992	C.E.E.03
772	17	August	1992	AF.30
773	26	August	1992	AS.23
774	26	August	1992	AS.08
775	28	August	1992	AF.36
776	14	September	1992	C.E.E.03
777	19	September	1992	C.E.E.12
778	2	October	1992	AS.23
779	6	October	1992	C.E.E.03
780	6	October	1992	C.E.E.03
781	9	October	1992	C.E.E.03
782	13	October	1992	AF.37
783	13	October	1992	AS.22
784	30	October	1992	C.L.A.C.10
785	30	October	1992	AF.34
786	10	November	1992	C.E.E.03
787	16	November	1992	C.E.E.03
788	19	November	1992	AF.38
789	25	November	1992	AS.08
790	25	November	1992	ME.03

Resolution No.	Date			Code
791	30	November	1992	C.L.A.C.10
792	30	November	1992	AS.22
793	30	November	1992	AF.34
794	3	December	1992	AF.36
795	11	December	1992	C.E.E.10
796	14	December	1992	AS.08
797	16	December	1992	AF.37
798	18	December	1992	C.E.E.03
799	18	December	1992	ME.05
800	8	January	1993	03
801	8	January	1993	03
802	25	January	1993	C.E.E.05
803	28	January	1993	ME.06
804	29	January	1993	AF.34
805	4	February	1993	05
806	5	February	1993	AS.23
807	19	February	1993	C.E.E.03
808	22	February	1993	C.E.E.06
809	2	March	1993	AF.06
810	8	March	1993	AS.22
811	12	March	1993	AF.34
812	12	March	1993	AF.44
813	26	March	1993	AF.38
814	26	March	1993	AF.36
815	30	March	1993	C.E.E.03
816	31	March	1993	C.E.E.03
817	7	April	1993	03
818	14	April	1993	AF.37
819	16	April	1993	C.E.E.04
820	17	April	1993	C.E.E.03
821	28	April	1993	C.E.E.12
822	30	April	1993	AS.28
823	30	April	1993	AF.34
824	6	May	1993	C.E.E.04
825	11	May	1993	AS.26
826	20	May	1993	AS.22
827	25	May	1993	C.E.E.06

Resolution No.	Date			Code
828	26	May	1993	03
829	26	May	1993	03
830	26	May	1993	ME.03
831	27	May	1993	AS.08
832	27	May	1993	C.L.A.C.10
833	27	May	1993	AS.23
834	1	June	1993	AF.34
835	2	June	1993	AS.22
836	4	June	1993	C.E.E.04
837	6	June	1993	AF.36
838	10	June	1993	C.E.E.04
839	11	June	1993	AS.08
840	15	June	1993	AS.22
841	16	June	1993	C.L.A.C.12
842	18	June	1993	C.E.E.10
843	18	June	1993	C.E.E.08
844	18	June	1993	C.E.E.04
845	18	June	1993	C.E.E.11
846	22	June	1993	AF.44
847	30	June	1993	C.E.E.03
848	8	July	1993	03
849	9	July	1993	AS.29
850	9	July	1993	AF.37
851	15	July	1993	AF.34
852	28	July	1993	ME.06
853	29	July	1993	AS.28
854	6	August	1993	AS.28
855	9	August	1993	C.E.E.09
856	10	August	1993	AF.38
857	20	August	1993	C.E.E.06
858	24	August	1993	AS.28
859	24	August	1993	C.E.E.04
860	27	August	1993	AS.22
861	27	August	1993	C.L.A.C.12
862	31	August	1993	C.L.A.C.12
863	13	September	1993	AF.37
864	15	September	1993	AF.34
865	22	September	1993	AF.36

Resolution No.	Date			Code
866	22	September	1993	AF.38
867	23	September	1993	C.L.A.C.12
868	29	September	1993	G.14
869	30	September	1993	C.E.E.03
870	1	October	1993	C.E.E.03
871	4	October	1993	C.E.E.03
872	5	October	1993	AF.44
873	13	October	1993	C.L.A.C.12
874	14	October	1993	AS.28
875	16	October	1993	C.L.A.C.12
876	19	October	1993	AS.28
877	21	October	1993	C.E.E.06
878	29	October	1993	AF.36
879	29	October	1993	AF.37
880	4	November	1993	AS.22
881	4	November	1993	AS.28
882	5	November	1993	AF.37
883	11	November	1993	AF.35
884	12	November	1993	AS.28
885	16	November	1993	AF.36
886	18	November	1993	AF.36
887	29	November	1993	ME.03
888	30	November	1993	C.L.A.C.10
889	15	December	1993	AS.08
890	15	December	1993	AF.34
891	20	December	1993	AF.44
892	22	December	1993	AS.28
893	6	January	1994	AF.44
894	14	January	1994	AF.30
895	28	January	1994	ME.06
896	31	January	1994	AS.28
897	4	February	1994	AF.36
898	23	February	1994	AF.37
899	4	March	1994	AS.23
900	4	March	1994	C.E.E.04
901	4	March	1994	AS.28
902	11	March	1994	AS.08

Resolution No.	Date			Code
903	16	March	1994	AF.34
904	18	March	1994	ME.05
905	23	March	1994	C.L.A.C.12
906	25	March	1994	AS.28
907	29	March	1994	AF.06
908	31	March	1994	C.E.E.03
909	5	April	1994	AF.44
910	14	April	1994	AF.39
911	21	April	1994	AF.38
912	21	April	1994	AF.44
913	22	April	1994	C.E.E.04
914	27	April	1994	C.E.E.03
915	4	May	1994	AF.39
916	5	May	1994	AF.37
917	6	May	1994	C.L.A.C.12
918	17	May	1994	AF.44
919	25	May	1994	AF.30
920	26	May	1994	C.L.A.C.10
921	26	May	1994	ME.03
922	31	May	1994	AF.34
923	31	May	1994	AF.36
924	1	June	1994	AS.25
925	8	June	1994	AF.44
926	13	June	1994	AF.39
927	15	June	1994	AS.08
928	20	June	1994	AF.44
929	22	June	1994	AF.44
930	27	June	1994	AF.30
931	29	June	1994	AS.25
932	30	June	1994	AF.34
933	30	June	1994	C.L.A.C.12
934	30	June	1994	AS.28
935	1	July	1994	AF.44
936	8	July	1994	C.E.E.06
937	21	July	1994	AS.28
938	28	July	1994	ME.06
939	29	July	1994	AS.08
940	31	July	1994	C.L.A.C.12

Resolution No.	Date			Code
941	23	September	1994	C.E.E.04
942	23	September	1994	C.E.E.04
943	23	September	1994	C.E.E.04
944	29	September	1994	C.L.A.C.12
945	29	September	1994	AF.34
946	30	September	1994	AF.36
947	30	September	1994	C.E.E.03
948	15	October	1994	C.L.A.C.12
949	15	October	1994	AS.23
950	21	October	1994	AF.38
951	21	October	1994	05
952	27	October	1994	AF.34
953	31	October	1994	AF.36
954	4	November	1994	AF.36
955	8	November	1994	AF.45
956	10	November	1994	10
957	15	November	1994	AF.37
958	19	November	1994	C.E.E.04
959	19	November	1994	C.E.E.04
960	21	November	1994	AF.37
961	23	November	1994	C.L.A.C.10
962	29	November	1994	ME.03
963	29	November	1994	03
964	29	November	1994	C.L.A.C.12
965	30	November	1994	AF.44
966	8	December	1994	AF.34
967	14	December	1994	C.E.E.03
968	16	December	1994	AS.30
969	21	December	1994	AS.08
970	12	January	1995	C.E.E.04
971	12	January	1995	AS.28
972	13	January	1995	AF.38
973	13	January	1995	AF.06
974	30	January	1995	ME.06
975	30	January	1995	C.L.A.C.12
976	8	February	1995	AF.42
977	22	February	1995	AF.44

Resolution No.	Date			Code
978	27	February	1995	AF.44
979	9	March	1995	05
980	22	March	1995	05
981	31	March	1995	C.E.E.03
982	31	March	1995	C.E.E.03
983	31	March	1995	C.E.E.03
984	11	April	1995	G.11
985	13	April	1995	AF.38
986	14	April	1995	AS.23
987	19	April	1995	C.E.E.04
988	21	April	1995	C.E.E.04
989	24	April	1995	AF.45
990	28	April	1995	C.E.E.05
991	28	April	1995	C.L.A.C.10
992	11	May	1995	C.E.E.07
993	12	May	1995	AS.28
994	17	May	1995	C.E.E.05
995	26	May	1995	AF.06
996	30	May	1995	ME.03
997	9	June	1995	AF.44
998	16	June	1995	C.E.E.03
999	16	June	1995	AS.30
1000	23	June	1995	AS.08
1001	30	June	1995	AF.38
1002	30	June	1995	AF.06
1003	5	July	1995	C.E.E.04
1004	12	July	1995	C.E.E.04
1005	17	July	1995	AF.44
1006	28	July	1995	ME.06
1007	31	July	1995	C.L.A.C.12
1008	7	August	1995	AF.42
1009	10	August	1995	C.E.E.05
1010	10	August	1995	C.E.E.04
1011	16	August	1995	AF.44
1012	28	August	1995	AF.49
1013	7	September	1995	AF.44
1014	15	September	1995	AF.38
1015	15	September	1995	C.E.E.04

Resolution No.	Date			Code
1016	21	September	1995	C.E.E.04
1017	22	September	1995	AF.06
1018	7	November	1995	05
1019	9	November	1995	C.E.E.03
1020	10	November	1995	AF.38
1021	22	November	1995	C.E.E.03
1022	22	November	1995	C.E.E.03
1023	22	November	1995	C.E.E.05
1024	28	November	1995	ME.03
1025	30	November	1995	C.E.E.05
1026	30	November	1995	C.E.E.04
1027	30	November	1995	C.E.E.10
1028	8	December	1995	AF.44
1029	12	December	1995	AF.44
1030	14	December	1995	AS.30
1031	15	December	1995	C.E.E.04
1032	19	December	1995	AS.08
1033	19	December	1995	AF.06
1034	21	December	1995	C.E.E.04
1035	21	December	1995	C.E.E.O4
1036	12	January	1996	AS.28
1037	15	January	1996	C.E.E.05
1038	15	January	1996	C.E.E.05
1039	29	January	1996	ME.06
1040	29	January	1996	AF.49
1041	29	January	1996	AF.38
1042	31	January	1996	AF.06
1043	31	January	1996	C.E.E.05
1044	31	January	1996	AF.40
1045	8	February	1996	AF.42
1046	13	February	1996	C.E.E.10
1047	29	February	1996	C.E.E.06
1048	29	February	1996	C.L.A.C.12
1049	5	March	1996	AF.49
1050	8	March	1996	AF.44
1051	27	March	1996	AS.23
1052	18	April	1996	ME.06

Resolution No.	Date			Code
1053	23	April	1996	AF.44
1054	26	April	1996	AF.40
1055	8	May	1996	AF.42
1056	29	May	1996	AF.06
1057	30	May	1996	ME.03
1058	30	May	1996	C.E.E.10
1059	31	May	1996	AF.38
1060	12	June	1996	AS.23
1061	14	June	1996	AS.30
1062	28	June	1996	AS.08
1063	28	June	1996	C.L.A.C.12
1064	11	July	1996	AF.42
1065	12	July	1996	AS.28
1066	15	July	1996	C.E.E.05
1067	26	July	1996	C.L.A.C.11
1068	30	July	1996	ME.06
1069	30	July	1996	C.E.E.05
1070	16	August	1996	AF.40
1071	30	August	1996	AF.38
1072	30	August	1996	AF.49
1073	28	September	1996	ME.05
1074	1	October	1996	C.E.E.03
1075	11	October	1996	AF.42
1076	22	October	1996	AS.19
1077	22	October	1996	AS.28
1078	9	November	1996	AF.46
1079	15	November	1996	C.E.E.05
1080	15	November	1996	AF.46
1081	27	November	1996	ME.03
1082	27	November	1996	C.E.E.10
1083	27	November	1996	AF.38
1084	27	November	1996	AF.06
1085	29	November	1996	C.L.A.C.12
1086	5	December	1996	C.L.A.C.12
1087	11	December	1996	AF.42
1088	12	December	1996	C.E.E.03
1089	13	December	1996	AS.30
1090	13	December	1996	12

Resolution No.	Date			Code
1091	13	December	1996	12
1092	23	December	1996	AS.08
1093	14	January	1997	C.E.E.05
1094	20	January	1997	C.L.A.C.10
1095	28	January	1997	ME.06
1096	30	January	1997	AS.28
1097	18	February	1997	AF.46
1098	27	February	1997	AF.42
1099	14	March	1997	AS.30
1100	27	March	1997	AF.38
1101	28	March	1997	C.E.E.13
1102	31	March	1997	AF.42
1103	31	March	1997	C.E.E.03
1104	8	April	1997	C.E.E.06
1105	9	April	1997	C.E.E.10
1106	16	April	1997	AF.42
1107	16	May	1997	C.E.E.03
1108	22	May	1997	AF.06
1109	28	May	1997	ME.03
1110	28	May	1997	C.E.E.10
1111	4	June	1997	AS.23
1112	12	June	1997	C.E.E.03
1113	12	June	1997	AS.30
1114	19	June	1997	C.E.E.13
1115	21	June	1997	AS.23
1116	27	June	1997	AF.38
1117	27	June	1997	AS.08
1118	30	June	1997	AF.42
1119	14	July	1997	C.E.E.05
1120	14	July	1997	C.E.E.05
1121	22	July	1997	G.15
1122	29	July	1997	ME.06
1123	30	July	1997	C.L.A.C.12
1124	31	July	1997	AS.28
1125	6	August	1997	AF.50
1126	27	August	1997	C.E.E.06
1127	28	August	1997	AF.43

Resolution No.	Date			Code
1128	12	September	1997	AS.30
1129	12	September	1997	AS.23
1130	29	September	1997	AF.42
1131	29	September	1997	AF.06
1132	8	October	1997	AF.51
1133	20	October	1997	AF.06
1134	23	October	1997	AS.23
1135	29	October	1997	AF.43
1136	6	November	1997	AF.50
1137	12	November	1997	AS.23
1138	14	November	1997	AS.30
1139	21	November	1997	ME.03
1140	28	November	1997	C.E.E.10
1141	28	November	1997	C.L.A.C.12
1142	4	December	1997	C.E.E.10
1143	4	December	1997	AS.23
1144	19	December	1997	C.E.E.03
1145	19	December	1997	C.E.E.05
1146	23	December	1997	AS.08
1147	13	January	1998	C.E.E.05
1148	26	January	1998	AF.06
1149	27	January	1998	AF.43
1150	30	January	1998	AS.28
1151	30	January	1998	ME.06
1152	5	February	1998	AF.50
1153	20	February	1998	AS.23
1154	2	March	1998	AS.23
1155	16	March	1998	AF.50
1156	16	March	1998	AF.51
1157	20	March	1998	AF.43
1158	25	March	1998	AS.23
1159	27	March	1998	AF.50
1160	31	March	1998	C.E.E.14
1161	9	April	1998	AF.44
1162	17	April	1998	AF.51
1163	17	April	1998	AF.06
1164	29	April	1998	AF.43

Resolution No.	Date			Code
1165	30	April	1998	AF.45
1166	13	May	1998	C.E.E.06
1167	14	May	1998	AS.30
1168	21	May	1998	C.E.E.03
1169	27	May	1998	ME.03
1170	28	May	1998	AF.52
1171	5	June	1998	AF.51
1172	6	June	1998	G.07
1173	12	June	1998	AF.42
1174	15	June	1998	C.E.E.03
1175	19	June	1998	AS.23
1176	24	June	1998	AF.43
1177	26	June	1998	AF.53
1178	29	June	1998	AS.08
1179	29	June	1998	AS.08
1180	29	June	1998	AF.43
1181	13	July	1998	AF.51
1182	14	July	1998	AF.50
1183	15	July	1998	C.E.E.04
1184	16	July	1998	C.E.E.03
1185	20	July	1998	AF.06
1186	21	July	1998	C.E.E.10
1187	30	July	1998	AS.29
1188	30	July	1998	ME.06
1189	13	August	1198	G.08
1190	13	August	1998	AF.43
1191	27	August	1998	C.E.E.06
1192	27	August	1998	AF.35
1193	28	August	1998	AS.19
1194	9	September	1998	AS.23
1195	15	September	1998	AF.43
1196	16	September	1998	AF.52
1197	18	September	1998	AF.52
1198	18	September	1998	AF. 06
1199	23	September	1998	C.E.E.14
1200	30	September	1998	AF.45
1201	15	October	1998	AF.50
1202	15	October	1998	AF.43

Resolution No.	Date			Code
1203	24	October	1998	C.E.E.14
1204	30	October	1998	AF.06
1205	5	November	1998	AS.23
1206	12	November	1998	AS.30
1207	17	November	1998	C.E.E.06
1208	19	November	1998	AF.52
1209	19	November	1998	AF.52
1210	24	November	1998	AS.23
1211	25	November	1998	ME.03
1212	25	November	1998	C.L.A.C.12
1213	3	December	1998	AF.43
1214	8	December	1998	AS.19
1215	17	December	1998	AF.06
1216	21	December	1998	AF.54
1217	22	December	1998	AS.08
1218	22	December	1998	AS.08
1219	31	December	1998	AF.43
1220	12	January	1999	AF.51
1221	12	January	1999	AF.43
1222	15	January	1999	C.E.E.05
1223	28	January	1999	ME.06
1224	28	January	1999	AF.06
1225	28	January	1999	AS.29
1226	29	January	1999	AF.53
1227	10	February	1999	AF.53
1228	11	February	1999	AF.06
1229	26	February	1999	AF.43
1230	26	February	1999	AF.50
1231	11	March	1999	AF.51
1232	30	March	1999	AF.06
1233	6	April	1999	AF.54
1234	9	April	1999	AF.48
1235	30	April	1999	AF.06
1236	7	May	1999	AS.31
1237	7	May	1999	AF.43
1238	14	May	1999	AF.06
1239	14	May	1999	C.E.E.14

Resolution No.	Date			Code
1240	15	May	1999	AS.30
1241	19	May	1999	AF.45
1242	21	May	1999	AS.23
1243	27	May	1999	ME.03
1244	10	June	1999	C.E.E.14
1245	11	June	1999	AF.51
1246	11	June	1999	AS.31
1247	18	June	1999	C.E.E.03
1248	25	June	1999	03
1249	25	June	1999	03
1250	29	June	1999	AS.08
1251	29	June	1999	AS.08
1252	15	July	1999	C.E.E.05
1253	28	July	1999	03
1254	30	July	1999	ME.06
1255	30	July	1999	AS.29
1256	3	August	1999	C.E.E.03
1257	3	August	1999	AS.31
1258	6	August	1999	AF.48
1259	11	August	1999	C.E.E.06/AF.45
1260	20	August	1999	AF.51
1261	25	August	1999	G.18
1262	27	August	1999	AS.31
1263	13	September	1999	AF.06
1264	15	September	1999	AS.31
1265	17	September	1999	G.20
1266	4	October	1999	AS.23
1267	15	October	1999	AS.19
1267	15	October	1999	AS.19
1268	15	October	1999	AF.43
1269	19	October	1999	G.07
1270	22	October	1999	AF.51
1271	22	October	1999	AF.50
1272	25	October	1999	AS.31
1273	5	November	1999	AF.48
1274	12	November	1999	AS.30
1275	19	November	1999	AS.23
1276	24	November	1999	ME.03

Resolution No.	Date			Code
1277	30	November	1999	C.L.A.C.12
1278	30	November	1999	05
1279	30	November	1999	AF.48
1280	3	December	1999	AS.23
1281	10	December	1999	AS.23
1282	14	December	1999	AF.06
1283	15	December	1999	AS.08
1284	17	December	1999	AS.23
1285	13	January	2000	C.E.E.05
1286	19	January	2000	AF.49
1287	31	January	2000	AS.29
1288	31	January	2000	ME.06
1289	7	February	2000	AF.51
1290	17	February	2000	03
1291	24	February	2000	AF.48
1292	29	February	2000	AF.06
1293	31	March	2000	AS.23
1294	13	March	2000	AF.43
1295	18	April	2000	AF.43
1296	19	April	2000	G.20
1297	12	May	2000	AF.53
1298	17	May	2000	AF.53
1299	19	May	2000	AF.51
1300	31	May	2000	ME.03
1301	31	May	2000	AF.06
1302	8	June	2000	AS.23
1303	14	June	2000	AS.08
1304	16	June	2000	AF.48
1305	21	June	2000	C.E.E.03
1306	5	June	2000	AF.51
1307	13	July	2000	C.E.E.05
1308	17	July	2000	G.26
1309	25	July	2000	AF.06
1310	27	July	2000	ME.06
1311	28	July	2000	AS.29
1312	31	July	2000	AF.53
1313	4	August	2000	AF.51

Resolution No.	Date			Code
1314	11	August	2000	G.18
1315	14	August	2000	AF.51
1316	23	August	2000	AF.48
1317	5	September	2000	AF.51
1318	7	September	2000	AF.56
1319	8	September	2000	AS.31
1320	15	September	2000	AF.53
1321	20	September	2000	AF.51
1322	7	October	2000	ME.06
1323	13	October	2000	AF.48
1324	30	October	2000	AF.06
1325	31	October	2000	G.27
1326	31	October	2000	03
1327	13	November	2000	G.28
1328	27	November	2000	ME.03
1329	30	November	2000	C.E.E.06/AF.45
1330	5	December	2000	AS.23
1331	13	December	2000	AS.08
1332	14	December	2000	AF.48
1333	19	December	2000	AS.19
1334	22	December	2000	AF.51

PART IV

THE COMPOSITION OF THE SECURITY COUNCIL (1946-2000)

Permanent Members:
China
France
Russian Federation
United Kingdom of Great Britain and Northern Ireland
United States of America

1946	*1947*	*1948*	*1949*
Australia	Australia	Argentina	Argentina
Brazil	Belgium	Belgium	Canada
Egypt	Brazil	Canada	Cuba
Mexico	Colombia	Colombia	Egypt
Netherlands	Poland	Syria	Norway
Poland	Syria	Ukrainian Soviet Socialist Republic	Ukrainian Soviet Socialist Republic

1950	*1951*	*1952*	*1953*
Cuba	Brazil	Brazil	Chile
Ecuador	Ecuador	Chile	Colombia
Egypt	India	Greece	Denmark
India	Netherlands	Netherlands	Greece
Norway	Turkey	Pakistan	Lebanon
Yugoslavia	Yugoslavia	Turkey	Pakistan

1954	*1955*	*1956*	*1957*
Brazil	Belgium	Australia	Australia
Colombia	Brazil	Belgium	Colombia
Denmark	Iran	Cuba	Cuba
Lebanon	New Zealand	Iran	Iraq
New Zealand	Peru	Peru	Philippines
Turkey	Turkey	Yugoslavia	Sweden

1958	*1959*	*1960*	*1961*
Canada	Argentina	Argentina	Ceylon
Colombia	Canada	Ceylon	Chile
Iraq	Italy	Ecuador	Ecuador
Japan	Japan	Italy	Liberia
Panama	Panama	Poland	Turkey
Sweden	Tunisia	Tunisia	United Arab Republic

1962

Chile
Ghana
Ireland
Romania
United Arab Republic
Venezuela

1963

Brazil
Ghana
Morocco
Norway
Philippines
Venezuela

1964

Bolivia
Brazil
Czechoslovakia
Ivory Coast
Morocco
Norway

1965

Bolivia
Ivory Coast
Jordan
Malaysia
Netherlands
Uruguay

1966

Argentina
Bulgaria
Japan
Jordan
Mali
Netherlands
New Zealand
Nigeria
Uganda
Uruguay

1967

Argentina
Brazil
Bulgaria
Canada
Denmark
Ethiopia
India
Japan
Mali
Nigeria

1968

Algeria
Brazil
Canada
Denmark
Ethiopia
Hungary
India
Pakistan
Paraguay
Senegal

1969

Algeria
Colombia
Finland
Hungary
Nepal
Pakistan
Paraguay
Senegal
Spain
Zambia

1970

Burundi
Colombia
Finland
Nepal
Nicaragua
Poland
Sierra Leone
Spain
Syria
Zambia

1971

Argentina
Belgium
Burundi
Italy
Japan
Nicaragua
Poland
Sierra Leone
Somalia
Syrian Arab Republic

1972

Argentina
Belgium
Guinea
India
Italy
Japan
Panama
Somalia
Sudan
Yugoslavia

1973

Australia
Austria
Guinea
India
Indonesia
Kenya
Panama
Peru
Sudan
Yugoslavia

1974

Australia
Austria
Byelorussian Soviet Socialist Republic

1975

Byelorussian Soviet Socialist Republic
Costa Rica
Guyana

1976

Benin
Guyana
Italy
Japan
Lybian Arab

1977

Benin
Canada
Germany, Federal Republic of

1974

Costa Rica
Indonesia
Iraq
Kenya
Mauritania
Peru
United
Republic of
Cameroon

1975

Iraq
Italy
Japan
Mauritania
Sweden
United
Republic of
Cameroon
United Republic of
Tanzania

1976

Republic
Pakistan
Panama
Romania
Sweden
United
Republic of
Tanzania

1977

India
Lybian Arab
Jamahiriya
Mauritius
Pakistan
Panama
Romania
Venezuela

1978

Bolivia
Canada
Czechoslovakia
Gabon
Germany
Federal
Republic of
India
Kuwait
Mauritius
Nigeria
Venezuela

1979

Bangladesh
Bolivia
Czechoslovakia
Gabon
Jamaica
Kuwait
Nigeria
Norway
Portugal
Zambia

1980

Bangladesh
German
Democratic
Republic
Jamaica
Mexico
Niger
Norway
Philippines
Portugal
Tunisia
Zambia

1981

German
Democratic
Republic
Ireland
Japan
Mexico
Niger
Panama
Philippines
Spain
Tunisia
Uganda

1982

Guyana
Ireland
Japan
Jordan
Panama
Poland
Spain
Togo
Uganda
Zaire

1983

Guyana
Jordan
Malta
Netherlands
Nicaragua
Pakistan
Poland
Togo
Zaire
Zimbabwe

1984

Burkina Faso
Egypt
India
Malta
Netherlands
Nicaragua
Pakistan
Peru
Ukrainian Soviet
Socialist Republic
Zimbabwe

1985

Australia
Burkina Faso
Denmark
Egypt
India
Madagascar
Peru
Thailand
Trinidad and
Tobago
Ukrainian Soviet
Socialist Republic

1986

Australia
Bulgaria
Congo
Denmark
Ghana
Madagascar
Thailand
Trinidad and Tobago
United Arab Emirates
Venezuela

1987

Argentina
Bulgaria
Congo
Germany, Federal Republic of
Ghana
Italy
Japan
United Arab Emirates
Venezuela
Zambia

1988

Algeria
Argentina
Brazil
Germany, Federal Republic of
Italy
Japan
Nepal
Senegal
Yugoslavia
Zambia

1989

Algeria
Brazil
Canada
Colombia
Ethiopia
Finland
Malaysia
Nepal
Senegal
Yugoslavia

1990

Canada
Colombia
Cuba
Ethiopia
Finland
Ivory Coast
Malaysia
Romania
Yemen
Zaire

1991

Austria
Belgium
Cuba
Ecuador
India
Ivory Coast
Romania
Yemen
Zaire
Zimbabwe

1992

Austria
Belgium
Cape Verde
Ecuador
Hungary
India
Japan
Morocco
Venezuela
Zimbabwe

1993

Brazil
Cape Verde
Djibouti
Hungary
Japan
Morocco
New Zealand
Pakistan
Spain
Venezuela

1994

Argentina
Brazil
Czech Republic
Djibouti
New Zealand
Nigeria
Oman
Pakistan
Rwanda
Spain

1995

Argentina
Botswana
Czech Republic
Germany
Honduras
Indonesia
Italy
Nigeria
Oman
Rwanda

1996

Botswana
Chile
Egypt
Germany
Guinea-Bissau
Honduras
Indonesia
Italy
Poland
Republic of Korea

1997

Chile
Costa Rica
Egypt
Guinea-Bissau
Japan
Kenya
Poland
Portugal
Republic of Korea
Sweden

1998	*1999*	*2000*
Bahrain	Argentina	Argentina
Brazil	Bahrain	Bangladesh
Costa Rica	Brazil	Canada
Gabon	Canada	Jamaica
the Gambia	Gabon	Malaysia
Japan	the Gambia	Mali
Kenya	Malaysia	Namibia
Portugal	Namibia	Netherlands
Slovenia	Netherlands	Tunisia
Sweden	Slovenia	Ukraine

NIJHOFF LAW SPECIALS

1. D. Campbell: *Abortion Law and Public Policy.* 1984 ISBN 90-247-3107-0
2. J. Pictet: *Development and Principles of International Humanitarian Law.* 1985 ISBN 90-247-3199-2
3. J. van Houtte: *Sociology of Law and Legal Anthropology in Dutch-speaking Countries.* 1985 ISBN 90-247-3175-5
4. C.D. De Fouloy: *Glossary of NAFTA Terms.* 1994 ISBN 0-7923-2719-5
5. H.L. Zielinski: *Health and Humanitarian Concerns.* Principles and Ethics. 1994 ISBN 0-7923-2963-5
6. K.S. Foster and D.C. Alexander: *Prospects of a US-Chile Free Trade Agreement.* 1994 ISBN 0-7923-2885-X
7. F.J.M. Feldbrugge (ed.): *Russian Federation Legislative Survey. June 1990-December 1992.* 1995 ISBN 0-7923-3243-1
8. R. Platzöder (ed.): *The 1994 United Nations Convention on the Law of the Sea.* Basic Documents with an Introduction. 1995 ISBN 0-7923-3271-7
9. D. Warner (ed.): *New Dimensions of Peacekeeping.* 1995 ISBN 0-7923-3301-2
10. M. van Leeuwen (ed.): *The Future of the International Nuclear Non-Proliferation Regime.* 1995 ISBN 0-7923-3433-7
11. E.-U. Petersmann: *International and European Trade and Environmental Law After the Uruguay Round.* 1995 ISBN 90-411-0857-2
12. V. Gowlland-Debbas: *The Problem of Refugees in the Light of Contemporary International Law Issues.* 1996 ISBN 90-411-0085-7
13. A. Kaczorowska: *International Trade Conventions and Their Effectiveness.* Present and Future. 1995 ISBN 0-7923-3362-4
14. T.F. Acuña: *The United Nations Mission in El Salvador.* A Humanitarian Law Perspective. 1995 ISBN 90-411-0123-3
15. H. Wiggering and A. Sandhövel (eds.): *European Environmental Advisory Councils.* 1996 ISBN 90-411-0873-4
16. E.A. Ankumah: *The African Commission on Human and Peoples' Rights.* Practice and Procedures. 1996 ISBN 90-411-0130-6
17. B. de Rossanet: *Peacemaking and Peacekeeping in Yugoslavia.* 1996 ISBN 90-411-0192-6
18. A. Webster and K. Packer (eds.): *Innovation and the Intellectual Property System.* 1996 ISBN 90-411-0907-2
19. H. Bocken and D. Ryckbost (eds.): *Codification of Environmental Law.* Draft Decree on Environmental Policy. 1996 ISBN 90-411-0911-0
20. K. Lescure and F. Trintignac: *International Justice for Former Yugoslavia.* The Working of the International Criminal Tribunal of the Hague. 1996 ISBN 90-411-0201-9
21. G. de Nooy (ed.): *The Role of European Naval Forces after the Cold War.* 1996 ISBN 90-411-0227-2
22. M. Bertrand and D. Warner (eds.): *A New Charter for a Worldwide Organisation?* 1997 ISBN 90-411-0286-8

NIJHOFF LAW SPECIALS

23. E.-U. Petersmann: *The GATTWTO Dispute Settlement System.* International Law, International Organizations and Dispute Settlement. 1996 ISBN 90-411-0933-1
24. G. de Nooy (ed.): *Cooperative Security, the OSCE, and its Code of Conduct.* 1996 ISBN 90-411-0316-3
25. M. Bertrand: *The United Nations.* Past, Present and Future. 1997 ISBN 90-411-0337-6
26. D. Dijkzeul: *The Management of Multilateral Organizations.* 1997 ISBN 90-411-0356-2
27. G. de Nooy (ed.): *The Role of European Ground and Air Forces after the Cold War.* 1997 ISBN 90-411-0397-X
28. M. Hilaire: *International Law and the United States Military Intervention in the Western Hemisphere.* 1997 ISBN 90-411-0399-6
29. D. Warner (ed.): *Human Rights and Humanitarian Law.* The Guest for Universality. 1997 ISBN 90-411-0407-0
30. J.C. Hathaway (ed.): *Reconceiving International Refugee Law.* 1997 ISBN 90-411-0418-6
31. G. de Nooy (ed.): *The Clausewitzian Dictum and the Future of Western Military Strategy.* 1997 ISBN 90-411-0455-0
32. Canadian Council on International Law and The Markland Group (ed.): *Treaty Compliance: Some Concerns and Remedies.* 1997 ISBN 90-411-0732-0
33. B. de Rossanet: *War and Peace in the Former Yugoslavia.* 1998 ISBN 90-411-0499-2
34. C.M. Mazzoni (ed.): *A Legal Framework for Bioethics.* 1998 ISBN 90-411-0523-9
35. M. Marín-Bosch: *Votes in the UN General Assembly.* 1998 ISBN 90-411-0564-6
36. L. Caflisch: *The Peaceful Settlement of Disputes between States: Universal and European Perspectives. Règlement pacifique des différends entre États: Perspectives universelle et européenne.* 1998 ISBN 90-411-0461-5
37. R. Wazir and N. van Oudenhoven (eds.): *Child Sexual Abuse: What can Governments do?* A Comparative Investigation into Policy Instruments Used in Belgium, Britain, Germany, the Netherlands and Norway. 1998 ISBN 90-411-1034-8
38. E.M. Barron and I. Nielsen (eds.): *Agriculture and Sustainable Land Use in Europe.* 1998 ISBN 90-411-9691-9
39. K. van Walraven (ed.): *Early Warning and Conflict Prevention.* 1998 ISBN 90-411-1064-X
40. S. Shubber: *The International Code of Marketing of Breast-milk Substitutes.* An International Measure to Protect and Promote Breast-feeding. 1999 ISBN 90-411-1100-X
41. G. Prins and H. Tromp (eds.): *The Future of War.* 2000 ISBN 90-411-1196-4
42. Choung Il Chee: *Korean Perspectives on Ocean Law Issues for the 21st Century.* 2000 ISBN 90-411-1301-0
43. K. Idris and M. Bartolo: *A Better United Nations for the New Millennium.* The United Nations System – How it is now and how it should be in the future. 2000 ISBN 90-411-1344-4

NIJHOFF LAW SPECIALS

44. E. McWhinney: *The United Nations and a New World Order for a New Millennium.* Self-determination, State Succession, and Humanitarian Intervention. 2000 ISBN 90-411-1371-1
45. C.Y. Pak: *Korea and the United Nations.* 2000 ISBN 90-411-1382-7
46. G. Prins and H. Tromp (eds.): *The Future of War.* 2000 ISBN 90-411-1399-1
47. V. Gowlland-Debbas, H. Hadj-Sahraoui and N. Hayashi (eds.): *Multilateral Treaty-making.* The Current Status of Challenges to and Reforms Needed in the International Legislative Process. 2000 ISBN 90-411-1448-3
48. G. Simpson (ed.): *Detainees Denied Justice.* 2001 ISBN 90-411-1552-8
49. C.A. Magariños, G. Assaf, S. Lall, J.D.-Martinussen, R. Ricupero and F. Sercovich: *Reforming the UN System.* UNIDO's Need Driven Model. 2001 ISBN 90-411-1669-9
50. K. Wellens (ed.): *Resolutions and Statements of the United Nations Security Council (1946-2000).* A Thematic Guide. 2001 ISBN 90-411-1722-9
51. P. Soar (ed.): *The New International Directory of Legal Aid.* 2001 ISBN 90-411-1718-0

MARTINUS NIJHOFF PUBLISHERS – THE HAGUE / BOSTON / LONDON

www.ingramcontent.com/pod-product-compliance
Lightning Source LLC
Chambersburg PA
CBHW061609180926
51615CB00006B/24
9789041117229